Keys to Buying
and Owning
a Home

Keys to Buying and Owning a Home

Jack P. Friedman, Ph.D., C.P.A., S.R.P.A.

New York · London · Toronto · Sydney

All inquiries should be addressed to:
Barron's Educational Series, Inc.
250 Wireless Boulevard
Hauppauge, New York 11788

Library of Congress Catalog Card No. 89-18314

International Standard Book No. 0-8120-4251-4

Library of Congress Cataloging in Publication Data

Friedman, Jack P.
   Keys to buying and owning a home / by Jack P. Friedman.
      p.   cm.—(Barron's business keys)
   Includes index.
   ISBN 0-8120-4251-4
   1. House buying.   2. Home ownership.   I. Title.   II. Series.
HD1379.F72   1990
643'.12—dc20   89-18314
                                                                                            CIP

PRINTED IN THE UNITED STATES OF AMERICA

0123 5500 987654321

CONTENTS

1

ADVANTAGES OF HOME OWNERSHIP

Approximately two out of three American families own the home they live in. Many renters would prefer to own but can't afford the necessary down payment or the carrying costs of ownership. So renters are typically people who can't afford ownership or don't want to make a long-term commitment to a particular area or dwelling. What are the attractive qualities of home ownership?

Physical. One's own home tends to be physically better than rental options. Homes are generally larger, have more interior space and more rooms, and provide opportunities to do things that are frequently prohibited for apartment dwellers, such as having pets, planting a garden, or playing musical instruments. Houses tend to offer more quiet and privacy than apartments. People tend to make improvements in their own home while their rental counterparts have little incentive to make improvements to their landlord's property.

Social. Neighbors become friends and help look

after one another's property. As a rule, home ownership increases one's involvement in one's neighborhood and community and increases concern over political and social matters, school systems, and local economic policies. Pride of ownership and an enhanced sense of responsibility are a part of home ownership.

Financial. Housing tends to be a good hedge against inflation, and because of the tendency toward inflation in our economy since World War II, housing has been an excellent investment. Mortgages are reduced through amortization—paying off the loan—so a home provides a form of forced savings.

Many families have found that a home provides the basis for financial security. For some, the sale of the family home has provided sufficient cash for a comfortable retirement.

Most homes can be purchased with only 20 percent or less of the price paid in cash; some people have even been able to borrow up to 100 percent of a home's price. Mortgage interest rates are perhaps the lowest of any form of consumer credit. Interest and real estate taxes can be deducted from one's federal and state taxable income by those who itemize these deductions, thus lowering the cost of housing.

Legal. Home ownership represents an important aspect of our legal system: private property rights. The owner is not subject to higher rents on each lease renewal, to eviction upon conversion to a condominium, or to eviction based on a minor infraction of a lease. The rights of an owner are well protected by the U.S. constitution. Although real property is subject to the government's right of eminent domain, a seizure or taking requires the payment of just compensation to the property owner.

2

DRAWBACKS OF OWNERSHIP

Home ownership isn't for everyone. There are distinct drawbacks, including often higher monthly costs in comparison to rentals, increased maintenance time and effort, and difficulty of a sale. If you are not reasonably settled in an area, that is, if you are likely to move within two to five years, home ownership may not be for you.

Comparing the rent on an apartment to the mortgage payment on a house is an oversimplification. You will probably spend much more on the house, both inside and out. You will probably select a better grade of carpet, linoleum, wallpaper, and curtains for the house you own than what your landlord puts in apartments. You will probably replace these items more frequently than a landlord would.

Your utility bills will probably be higher because of increased heated space, and you will pay all costs whereas your landlord probably paid at least the water and sewer bills. When something goes wrong, you, not the landlord, pay for the plumber, electrician, or carpenter. Even if you do the job yourself, your time has value and the parts cost money (although some people gain great satisfaction from doing their own repair work). You will pay for the paint and painter, and either maintain your own lawn or hire someone to do it. You will buy the necessary tools for all jobs, except the ones you borrow from a neighbor or rent. Even basic yard maintenance can require expensive tools and chemicals; so expect to spend more than for an apartment.

Your house may not be as convenient as your apartment to work, necessitating additional transportation costs—frequently a longer, more expensive commute or another vehicle. So, when comparing costs, include all home ownership costs, not just the ones paid to your lender.

Real estate is like a mousetrap—easy to get into but hard to get out of. A house can sell the same day it goes up for sale, or it can remain on the market for many months. In the extreme situation of a depressed or overbuilt local economy, a house may not sell for years. All in all, however, most houses offered at market price do sell within 90 days. Sales expenses include a brokerage commission (5 to 7 percent), title and legal fees (up to 1 percent), and often loan charges to prepay your mortgage or to help the buyer arrange financing (1 to 4 percent). Total selling costs can easily approach or exceed 10 percent of the home's price. If housing inflation is 5 percent annually, it will take you at least two years to recover these costs. So, if you don't expect to be in a home for two years or longer, save yourself the costs and aggravation of a quick resale. There are exceptions, of course, if your employer moves you around and pays your relocation costs.

3

LOCATION CONSIDERATIONS

For many people, where a home is can be as important as what the house itself offers in size, style, and amenities. These location considerations reflect the needs of the all occupants. If you're part of a family with children, or a couple expecting to start a family, nearness to schools and the quality of the school district typically come first. Then comes proximity to shopping, churches, and other family activities; finally comes commutation to work. For most people, travel *time* is more important than travel *distance*.

Specific location considerations include price, school districts, neighborhoods, municipal government, transportation system, and religious, cultural, and retail proximity.

Price. Prices in some locales may be above your means. You must rule out the unaffordable.

School districts. Small communities may have only one school or one school district to serve the entire area, but you will have more choice if you live in a city. Generally, such a densely populated area is surrounded by many suburbs, each with its own school system, thus providing a wide variety of places from which to select. The dominant city in the area will offer a number of elementary, junior high, and high schools, though busing to achieve racial integration is likely to mean that your children may not go to the school nearest your home. To find the best school, ask these questions:

- Does the district attract and retain good teachers?
- What percentage of local graduates go on to college?
- What is the rating of students in the local system on national achievement tests?
- What is the general level of education of the local citizenry?
- What is the response of the local citizenry to school tax levies?
- How much is spent per child, compared to other systems?
- Is there a well-developed local vocational education system?

Neighborhoods. Many people want to live in an area where they will be part of the dominant majority. This may refer to financial status or to age, national origin, or religion. Such a desire is not discriminatory—excluding minorities from that area would be. You might want to be close to certain retail establishments or to be near other people who share a similar religion or values. For example, if you're of Irish descent and want to live in Boston among those of similar ancestry, your choice of neighborhoods will be wide—but more limited than if your selection was not limited by this consideration. If you're a minority—say of Chinese descent living in Boston—and wish to live mainly among others of Chinese descent, your neighborhood choices in Boston will be narrow.

Municipal government. The city or town that you

seek should reflect your preferences. Its spending policy (police and fire protection, garbage collection, municipal hospitals, libraries, parks), political leadership, tax base, and economic situation may be important. If you want extensive services, expect high taxes.

Transportation system. If you or your spouse relies on public transportation to get to and from work or routine shopping, rule out any place where the system is inadequate. Long commutes to work can be tiresome, whether in your automobile or in a bus or train. You might wish to time the commute during peak traffic hours before making a commitment to a certain area; in addition, investigate the total costs of commutation.

Religious, cultural, and retail proximity. Nearness to a particular place of worship or cultural center may be a key criterion. Often it is important to be near a hospital or shopping center. While some prefer to live away from any traffic generator, others might find it essential to be able to walk to shopping.

4

INTERIOR SPACE

First, decide how much space you need, its required configuration, and how much you can afford. After you have narrowed the possibilities, you can focus on floor plans.

Square footage. The typical three-bedroom, two-bath house built within the last 20 years has between 1200 and 1900 square feet of heated livable area. This includes a living or family room, kitchen, and dining room or area. Smaller homes will be "missing" a room or have very small rooms. Larger homes will have more spacious rooms or an "extra" room. A four-bedroom home generally has 1600 to 2500 square feet, and those with more rooms will be larger. A house under 1200 will probably be described as small, while more than 2500 will be large. One over 3000 will be large by most standards.

Square footage is generally measured by exterior (outside) dimensions but there may be inconsistencies in reporting owing to mistake, misrepresentation, improper counting (including an attached garage), or local custom (in some places a fraction of covered patios is included in the total). In many areas prices are noted on a per-square-foot basis—a low price per square foot may seem like a bargain. However, don't accept someone's word for the size—verify it yourself, or put in the contract that if it doesn't "measure out," the price will be reduced.

Interior configuration. The number of bedrooms and bathrooms you need depends on how many people you need to house. If you're just starting a family, consider your needs for at least five years. Sometimes they'll be no problem—but don't count on it. A family of four can easily fit into a three-bedroom house, unless the children are of different sexes and each must have a separate room, and, at the same time, an extra bedroom is needed for an office, study, or guest room. The same family of four could easily get by with two bathrooms. However, a family of five or six would probably have fewer problems in mornings and evenings if there were two sinks in each bathroom. Write down the minimum number of rooms you need now and in the foreseeable future, as it will help narrow your search. Although adding a room at a later date is possible for most houses, financing and inconvenience can make this difficult.

Size of rooms. Even when your budget dictates the overall size of a house, you need to be mindful of the size of each room. Will your furniture fit? Is the living or family room suitable for your entertainment needs? Is the dining area of adequate size for family or entertainment needs? What size beds will you need for each bedroom, and will they fit comfortably where needed? Be sure to check whether window and door location might restrict furniture placement. Are cabinets, closets, and other storage areas, including the attic, adequate? Are there built-in shelves or desks that seem to add space?

Levels. Do you want a one- or two-story house, a split level or bi-level? Two stories are perhaps 5 percent less expensive to build than one, tend to be less expensive to operate, and allow more exterior land. However, they are entirely unsuitable for the elderly and handicapped. Many modern two-story homes are built with the master bedroom down and children's rooms up so the kids won't interfere with entertaining guests. However, if you have infants or toddlers, you may find the stairway inconvenient, especially at night.

Floor plans. Each house has its own traffic pattern. Your main entrance should lead people into the living room and be easily accessible from the driveway or street. A second entrance through the utility room or kitchen with a sheltered walkway to the driveway is also desirable. This entrance can be used for bringing in groceries and wet or muddy children.

The room arrangement of the house should allow you to go from any room to any other room without passing through a third room. The living room should be isolated from the normal traffic flow of the house to permit undisturbed conversation or entertainment. Routes between all rooms in the house and the outdoor areas should be short and direct (especially important in case of fire).

The kitchen ideally will have access to the outdoor patio (for carrying packages in and trash out, and for outdoor cooking convenience). It could also have a window to the backyard so the cook, when inside, can keep an eye on small children playing. In addition, the kitchen should be laid out so that there is an efficient working arrangement between the oven, refrigerator, sink, dishwasher, cabinets, and dining area(s).

A perfect house has not yet been built, so don't expect to find everything just right. But here are some specifics to seek in a floor plan:

- The front door should open to a hall or foyer rather than the living room.
- There should be a coat closet near the front door.
- Bedrooms and bathrooms should not be directly

visible from the foyer, living room, or dining room.
- Windows and doors in rooms should not cause awkward furniture placement.
- There should be easy access from parking area(s) to the house.
- Closets should be placed between rooms to reduce noise.

5

THE EXTERIOR

The style and materials used for a home say something about its owner, just as the way one dresses offers insight into one's personality or character. There are three parts to the overall exterior appearance of a home: style, materials, and landscaping.

Style. Houses come in numerous styles ranging from traditional to contemporary, from Oriental to Georgian. Styles give certain impressions; for example, houses with columns like the White House give the impression that a decision maker lives there. Contemporary styles give the impression of a modern lifestyle. Some homes have "curb appeal," brokers' language meaning that prospective buyers who drive by will like them enough to look inside.

Home buyers must look past the facade because beauty is only skin deep—a fabulous home may be bargain priced because it lacks curb appeal, but that can often be improved with low-cost cosmetics (paint, landscaping, shutters). Before buying, be sure that the appearance is suitable for your needs or that it can be corrected without great expense.

Materials. Building materials for the exterior of a

home will vary depending upon climate, styles, costs, housing codes, and subdivision restrictions. Brick tends to be maintenance-free, although doors, eaves, and trim are typically wood. Any exterior wood needs painting every three to ten years depending on climate and quality of materials. Aluminum siding is relatively maintenance-free.

Roofing materials have a limited useful life—typically 10 to 25 years, again depending on the climate and quality. The longevity of different kinds of fences will vary for the same reason. So don't expect any house to be maintenance-free.

Landscaping. Landscaping can cost several thousand dollars, considering grading, sod, shrubbery and tree planting, and pruning. An underground automatic sprinkler system is essential in some parts of the country. Spend some time inspecting the exterior of the house you're buying to check its current condition and to see what changes you will have to make.

Garage. Ideally, the garage should be on the side of the house most exposed to winter wind or summer heat. Avoid blocking prevailing warm-weather breezes. A two-car garage should have a 16-foot-wide door as a minimum; 18 feet is preferable. The garage floor should slope one to two inches toward the door so that water will not stand. If the laundry area is in the garage, it should be elevated for proper drainage. Slope the driveway toward the street a minimum of one-eighth inch per foot of paving. Try to assure that the design of your garage complements that of your house. If you do not need a garage for storage, a carport is adequate, especially in moderate climates.

6

LOT OR SITE CONSIDERATIONS

Prospective home buyers spend most of their time evaluating the house and its immediate neighborhood, paying little or no attention to the property as a whole, especially the lot on which the house is built. This is a mistake. Important considerations for the specific lot or site include deed restrictions, size and shape, utilities, topography, orientation, the presence of traffic and noise, parking, and zoning. How much each matters depends on your individual preferences.

Restrictive covenants. Developers use deed restrictions to control building activities in subdivisions. These restrictive covenants regulate such things as size, style, and location of structures as well as the quality, cost, and design of any improvements. The activity of the owners may also be restricted. For example, certain commercial enterprises may be prohibited in residential areas. These covenants serve to protect the homeowner by assuring minimum house sizes, uniformity, quality of housing, and absence of commercialism. To be enforceable, restrictions must be reasonable, not immoral or illegal, and not contrary to public policy.

Size and shape. The preferred lot size varies with the local area. Large lots are considered more desirable (i.e., sell for a higher price) than small ones in most places despite greater maintenance requirements. Your personal preference might be the opposite. At one time, corner lots were held to be desirable, but recent studies have not confirmed this. Instead, inside lots, because they are exposed to less traffic and noise, may be preferable. In the Northeast, a 50-foot-wide lot is perfectly acceptable, whereas in the South and West greater width is the norm. The depth may matter to you if you plan to add a pool or construct extensive decking, or if you need play areas for children or running room for pets.

Setback. Minimum setbacks for the front and side yards are set by city codes. The house you are considering ought to be in conformance with whatever requirements existed when it was built. If standards have since been upgraded, existing homes are unaffected.

Utilities. Consider water (is it drinkable and does it have adequate pressure?), electricity, natural gas, and sanitary sewerage. Would it be acceptable if one or more were minimal or absent? Cost is a factor. For instance, electric homes are expensive to operate in the winter but many find them quite acceptable. Homes on septic systems may be perfectly adequate, although you may be assessed for sewer lines and connections at a later date. If a home is missing a facility that you consider essential, strike it.

Topography. A perfectly flat lot may not provide adequate drainage. Be sure that the ground slopes so as to divert water away from the house. Lots with steep slopes are hard to build on and to drive into. They should be avoided or corrected before building, unless an intelligent building design can take advantage of the situation.

Orientation. An energy-conscious buyer will want the major glass areas of the house to face south. The winter sun will come in, but, provided the overhang is adequate, the summer sun won't.

Traffic and noise. If traffic is or can be expected to be heavy or fast, or if many commercial vehicles use the streets in the area, consider whether the location fits your expected lifestyle. If you have or expect children, you'll want them to be safe and to save yourself from worries. When children are not a consideration, you might not object and so might find a real bargain. In fact, some buyers seek out busy places expecting ultimate commercial use for their property and hence a highly profitable resale. But if the safety of your children is paramount, seek a quiet or dead-end street.

Parking. With two- and three-car families commonplace, judge the adequacy of parking and driveways. Narrow front yards may dictate a driveway wide enough for only one car at a time. If the standards in the neighborhood are for two car widths, the price of the lot should reflect the inadequacy.

Zoning. This is a municipal ordinance regulating the use of land. All major cities in the United States use zoning except Houston, Texas. It is a good idea to be sure the property is zoned for the use intended, i.e., a single-family home. More important, check the zoning of surrounding property, especially if vacant, to be sure that allowed uses are compatible with your home.

7

CONDOMINIUMS AND COOPERATIVES

There are various ways of dividing the ownership of real estate. To allow buyers with limited funds to enjoy the benefits of owning property, it is often necessary to have the type of shared ownership offered by condominium or cooperative setups.

A condominium, or "condo," combines individual and collective ownership. The owner has title to a unit within a building or complex and shared ownership of the rest of the property. For example, in a high-rise condo apartment building, each owner controls a dwelling unit in the building. The hallways, elevators, basement, lobby, grounds, and recreation areas are shared and owned in common by all unit owners. Units are sold just like any other property, and each owner may finance his or her purchase with a separate mortgage loan. There is some type of owners' association that collects fees to pay for maintenance and other costs connected with the common property.

Condo owners are subject to a set of bylaws covering how the property may be used.

A **co-op** is similar to a condo, but the legal setup is different. The purchaser of a co-op does not receive title to the property, which is owned by a special-purpose corporation. The purchaser receives certain shares in the corporation that permit the use of a unit in the building. The costs of running the building, including debt service on the mortgage loan used to buy the building, are shared among the owners. Shares in a unit may be sold on the market, but the corporation, by vote of the shareholders, can decide on who may purchase and occupy the unit. Therefore, shares in a co-op are not as liquid as units in a condo. Co-ops are used primarily for high-rise residential buildings, particularly in New York City.

One of the keys to making a sound investment in a co-op or condo is to buy at the initial offering of a new building or a conversion from a rental. Usually existing tenants are offered an "insider's" price, typically 25 percent less than the price offered to the market. An astute person might be able to buy at an attractive price even if it is more than the insider's price.

8

BUILDING YOUR
NEW HOME

Reasons for building a new home include getting exactly what you want (or what you think you want), building on the lot you already own, and getting something brand-new.

Drawbacks include the time and annoyance of the process and, typically, a higher cost than for comparable existing housing. A used home is likely to be located in an established area where the character of the neighborhood is apparent, and it will have an established yard with trees and shrubs. However, it may be lacking in certain critical features and could require more maintenance than a brand-new house. For example, adequate insulation is not found in many homes more than 15 years old, and some homes do not have adequate electrical wiring to handle today's household appliances.

Not all house plans fit on all lots: to the contrary, a given plan will probably not fit on a randomly selected lot. It is difficult to find the lot for your dream home—much simpler to buy a lot that you like and then to look for a suitable house plan.

You may find that the deed restrictions or restrictive covenants on the lot are highly desirable for you and will protect your interests, or you may find that you cannot comply with them. For example, if a subdivision is restricted to a minimum size house of 3,000 square feet with 50 percent or more brick facade, you may feel well protected. However, if that's not what you planned, then you will have to find another lot more suitable.

The building business is full of people who are as honest as the day is long—but there are also those who will steal from anyone. Finding a good builder doesn't have to be a hit-or-miss proposition. Ask people who own homes that you admire. Find out whether the home turned out as expected and whether the builder was good to work with. Another approach is to inspect new homes—when you find one that is well made, interview the builder and ask for the names of owners of other homes he has built. Check those references. Find out which bank finances his construction loans and how it evaluates him. If a license is required, ascertain that he is so licensed. Check with the local Better Business Bureau for any complaints filed.

There are three major types of home-building contracts:

Fixed price. This requires the builder to complete the project for a specific dollar amount. If the actual construction cost is less than the contract price, the builder gets to keep all the difference; on the other hand, if the cost exceeds the bid, the builder absorbs the loss.

Guaranteed maximum price. The buyer pays for only the actual cost incurred (including a builder's fee) within the maximum price guarantee. Builder and buyer share in any savings between the actual cost and maximum price.

Cost plus. Under this method, the builder is paid for actual costs incurred plus an additional percentage or fixed amount. This type of contract is frequently used when time is critical or the exact nature of the completed project is not known when the contract is signed. However, the owner has additional risk because the builder has no incentive to minimize costs.

There are several questions to be raised in selecting a builder. Does he have prior experience building similar houses? Can he provide the names of those customers, along with original cost estimates and the actual cost of each house? Does he have experience in the local area? Will he be responsible for specific performance—that is, for fulfilling all the terms of the contract? Who are the subcontractors to be used for each major activity area? What is their reputation for quality and reliability? What is their relationship with the builder?

Generally, a local builder has advantages over an outsider. He knows the building regulations, labor supplies, and sources of materials. A builder not familiar with local conditions may run into conflicts, time delays, or greater expenses. Also, it is easier to check the references of a local builder.

Finally, unless the builder has an extremely good reputation, you should require the builder to post a performance bond to guarantee the job to completion in the event that he doesn't finish it in good order.

9

WHETHER TO USE A BROKER

A broker is typically paid by the home seller, so at least according to contracts a buyer incurs no cost by using a broker. There is a small but growing trend for buyers to hire their own broker to find exactly what they are looking for and to negotiate the lowest price. This is the exception, perhaps accounting for only 1 to 2 percent of all residential transactions.

As a practical matter, most buyers and sellers make their deal through a real estate broker. For buyers, the reasons for this include: being unfamiliar with the homebuying process, under time pressure to buy, looking within a fairly large area, or in need of extensive market information to make a decision. By contrast, if you are looking to buy in a limited geographical area that you know quite well, you might be able to identify all suitable properties by yourself. Driving through subdivisions and looking at newspaper advertisements are two popular ways of finding properties.

There is no doubt that a broker can be efficient.

There is much more choice in a large city than a small one, and many more factors to consider. You may need a broker to help narrow your search.

There is a notion that a property offered for sale by its owner will be a bargain. This is not necessarily so. Often sellers are unwilling to pay a commission to a broker, or to anyone else—not even the buyer in the form of a lower selling price. Generally speaking, the average seller is not as close to the market as the average salesman or broker, and therefore may offer the property at too high or too low a price. If you are knowledgeable about prices and read the real estate ads regularly, you might land a bargain. But don't count on it.

Some people make fast decisions on limited information, whereas others are more cautious. If you are the type to require all possible information for this important decision, you'll probably contact several brokers.

Here are some specific services a professional real estate broker should be able to provide for you:

- Provide up-to-date information on what's available in the market
- Show you neighborhoods with homes in your price range
- Provide current information on zoning, growth, tax assessments, schools, and availability of stores, services, and transportation
- Arrange appointments
- Help you evaluate exterior and interior features of various homes—the good and the bad—so you'll find a home that fits your needs and tastes.

A broker also puts you in touch with appraisers, engineers, lawyers, and insurance agents, if and when their services are needed. And finally, a broker can provide information on financing and assistance in arranging your mortgage.

As a legal matter, the broker typically works for

the seller—the commission comes out of the seller's proceeds from the house sale. But in reality a broker's income is generated by sales, and so their interests lie in making deals work. A good broker or sales agent is skilled at bringing buyer and seller together to make a sale that satisfies everyone. Furthermore, the broker is legally obligated to treat everyone fairly.

10

SELECTING AN AGENT OR BROKER

To understand who's who in real estate brokerage, you need to learn the following terminology.

Brokers and salespersons. These individuals must be licensed by the state. In most states a *salesperson* must be sponsored by a broker, which means that the broker is responsible for the salesperson, earnest (deposit) money, and any other matters. The *broker* collects the commission on a sale and pays the salespersons who effect the sale some fraction of it—often 50 percent.

To earn a salesperson's license, one must pass a multiple-choice test mainly concerned with legal matters of real estate and agency law (not salesmanship) and take courses totaling 30, 60, or more clock hours, depending on state law. After holding a sales license for a period of time set by law (often two or three years) and receiving some more education, a salesperson is eligible for a broker's license. The broker's test is slightly more comprehensive and complex than the sales examinations. Brokers and salespersons together may be referred to as *licensees*. Sometimes they are called *agents*, especially salespersons, who are called *sales agents*.

Commissions. Nearly all brokers and salespersons are independent contractors (they work for themselves) and are paid via commissions earned by sales. The agreement to sell is with the property owner, to whom they owe loyalty. Their income is dependent on the number and dollar value of the sales they make. Legally, they must be fair to you, and they want you to be happy with them and the house you buy. This will enhance their reputation, which is their most valuable asset. The state board that regulates licensees is called the Real Estate Commission. (Obviously, the word *commission* here takes on a meaning that has nothing to do with fees paid for selling property.)

REALTOR®. This trade name can be used only by a broker or salesperson who is a member of the National Association of REALTORS®. This organization sponsors state and local chapters throughout the United States. Members must subscribe to a Code of Ethics which distinguishes them from other licensees. Approximately one-third of all licensees are REALTORS®. Most of the active real estate licensees are REALTORS®, but note that having a license is not enough to make one a REALTOR®.

Franchises. Local branches of firms are owned by individuals who pay $10,000 or so to acquire the franchise name. In addition, they pay about 6 percent of all commissions earned to the franchise organization, and they pay for their own local advertising. While there is standardization of advertising and appearance, each firm is independently owned and operated.

Multiple Listing Services (MLS). In most areas, the real estate brokers belong to an MLS. Members agree to pool all of their listings, which gives all members access to all listings. Consequently, any member has information on all properties listed by all members. A few brokerage firms are so large, with so many listings, that they need not join, but nearly all other firms find that the MLS helps their sales and provides a much wider range of houses to their clients.

Selection. Real estate brokers can help you find the right house if you're prepared to use their services wisely. The person you select to help you buy a home must be licensed. He or she need not be a REALTOR®, though you will find that most who are active in the business are. Real estate brokers need not be franchised, although some people have more confidence in a franchised firm. Make sure, however, that they have access to enough listings to serve your needs. Most of all, check their reputation and references. Then visit several of them to find out what houses are available in your price range. Let them know what you want in a house—its size, cost, quality, and neighborhood. Review their listings and take notes on the houses you like. Visit as many houses as necessary, and, most important, ask plenty of questions. Professional brokers will tell you about the drawbacks of a house as well as its assets, but it helps to ask knowledgeable questions. A broker gets paid a percentage of the sales price and is willing to provide many services for this commission. Even though the commission is paid by the seller, the buyer benefits from many of these services.

11

SELECTING HOUSES TO INSPECT

You will probably want to inspect at least five houses, perhaps more than 20, before making an offer on any. The number depends on the time you have to spend, your temperament, and how much information you need to make a decision. House-hunting trips take time and can be stressful unless you are great at reading maps and have no children to tag along.

Use a systematic and disciplined approach in selecting homes to visit. Get a good map and a notebook or clipboard. Rule out towns, neighborhoods, or subdivisions that you don't want, and circle those that you do. Use the telephone effectively. Get exact locations. Repeat them back to be sure your notes are correct. Do the same for directions. Write clearly. Make appointments and cluster times together with locations, but allow enough time to inspect each home and area, to eat meals, and to make up for wrong turns on unfamiliar streets.

When on the phone with an owner, agent, or builder, ask for a description of the house to be sure you have not ruled it out previously. Reasons might be the number of stories, its age, location, school district, number of bathrooms or bedrooms, and price. If you want your children to walk to school, or if shopping must be within walking distance, be sure that the location is appropriate. Don't waste precious time on anything you've ruled out.

Brokers who are members of an MLS probably have access to a computer that can selectively search all listings based on certain criteria. Give them a price range, size range in square feet, and minimum number of bedrooms and bathrooms, for example, and they can print out a list of all homes that meet your criteria. If the list is too long, add more criteria, such as the age, number of stories, garage requirements, or location. If there are few listings—say five or fewer—inspect all. Then loosen some of your criteria to see more. The computer may also print out a list of properties that have sold in the past year. This can offer very helpful information as to price trends and the relative value of homes, a major negotiating tool.

When you are looking at a number of homes on the same day, they can easily "run together" in your mind; that is, features of one become associated with those of another. This is where taking good notes come in. Do you have an instant camera? This can supplement your notes. A camcorder is even better. With it you can talk and shoot at the same time. (Of course, ask the owner or broker for permission before taping anything.) Identify each house adequately on the tape. When you return to your motel (or home or apartment) you can review the tape to reinforce your memory, or send the tape to your spouse or parent if he or she is out of town but helping to make a decision.

12

DISCRIMINATION IN HOUSING

It is the policy of the United States government to provide, within constitutional limitations, for fair housing throughout the nation.

Housing. It is unlawful, on the basis of race, color, religion, sex, national origin, disability or familial status:

- To refuse to sell or rent or refuse to negotiate the sale or rental of a dwelling;
- To discriminate in terms, conditions, or privileges of a sale or rental of a dwelling;
- To advertise or print anything that would be discriminatory with respect to the sale or rental of a dwelling;
- To represent a unit as being unavailable for inspection; or
- To induce anyone to sell or rent concerning neighborhood entry of an ethnic group.

Amendments to the Fair Housing Act that were introduced in 1989 allow punitive damages to those who are adversely affected. So, fines can be substantial, whereas in the past the fine could be $1,000 or less.

Lending. It is illegal for any bank, savings and loan association, insurance company, mortgage broker, or other firm in the lending business to practice discrimination. They may not charge more interest or offer unequal terms or conditions for purchasing, building, improving, or maintaining a dwelling.

Of course, all who apply for a mortgage loan are subject to a credit check. And their income is subject to review to determine if it qualifies them for the amount they seek to borrow. Consequently, before you begin to look for a new home, make sure that your credit has been established, and clear up any problems that are apparent in a credit report. Everyone must have good credit and an adequate income in order to qualify for a mortgage loan.

13

HUSBAND AND WIFE HOME-BUYING PRACTICES

Decision-making process. Recent studies reveal something about the negotiating process that married couples go through when they make any decision. It was once believed that one spouse was dominant in the real estate decision-making process, but some recent studies indicate that most people are willing to reject any house not acceptable to their spouse. Instances of a spouse trying to be dominant in the home-buying process are more likely to occur among relatively inexperienced buyers.

Commonly, one spouse gives in to the other to avoid conflict. Home buying is such an important decision that spouses will not insist on a house that they know will be unsatisfactory to their mate. Couples in the market for a new home are often under pressure to buy soon, but they still try to keep each other happy. Couples should talk about their preferences regarding homes. An open evaluation makes home buying a more satisfying experience.

Financing. In the past, many mortgage lenders would not consider a working wife's income on a mortgage application, nor would they lend to a single woman or female head of the family. Fortunately, these discriminatory practices are against the law now, and qualified women—as well as qualified working couples—may obtain mortgage loans. Furthermore, lending institutions must now consider both incomes and make their decisions on the individual merits of each application.

The wife's employment history, stability, and earning ability are evaluated by the same standard as the husband's. However, in developing a budget for your family, it is not wise to include either spouse's income if there is a possibility of one resigning from work to take care of children or attend school. If both incomes are needed for house payments and one is lost, severe financial strain could result.

Dividing Marital Property. Statistics indicate that more than a third of marriages in the United States end in divorce. Eventual division of the property is therefore a possibility we must all consider. When real estate is involved, this process can be not only unpleasant but also complex. State law or courts may dictate who gets which assets in a divorce. The situation can lead to lengthy legal battles and great expense to either or both parties. Disputes about property ownership may be avoided by using certain legal devices. These include premarital agreements, the partitioning of property during the marriage, selecting the preferred form of joint ownership (with legal consultation) and keeping accurate records to prevent commingling separate and community property in community property states. Well-defined property ownership within the marriage can minimize the court costs of a divorce and preserve good feelings between the parties.

14

DECIDING HOW MUCH TO OFFER

After you have decided that a certain house appears to be suitable for your family, the next step is to make an offer. You can offer the asking price and the seller's terms to assure purchase, but asking prices are often inflated to leave negotiating room. Negotiating is expected, even if you feel uncomfortable about this activity. Keys 20, 21, and 22 provide more information on negotiation.

What you really need to know is the market value of the property. Real estate appraisers are expert in estimating this amount, but you might not have the time to wait for this information or care to pay a $200-$300 fee when you don't know whether you will buy the property. Your lender, however, will insist on an appraisal before making the loan. Therefore, when submitting an offer, you can include a requirement that the property must appraise for at least the amount in your contract or you need not buy it.

You still need a good idea of what the property is worth so that your offer will not be foolishly high or embarrassingly low. In the shopping process, you probably developed an idea of its worth in comparison to other properties. In addition, many multiple listing services have a "Sold" book that lists or pictures properties sold in the past month or quarter. It typically provides all the information for that house from the "For Sale" book, plus the selling price, financing terms, and time on the market before sale. Your broker may lend you these informative books as the information is typically not guarded as is the "For Sale" book.

Market trends may also be a factor in deciding how much to offer. When the market is rising rapidly, you might offer the full amount to be certain of purchase; in a falling market, you might find a real bargain by making a low offer to an anxious or desperate seller. Still, market value provides the benchmark amount by which offers are judged.

Professional real estate appraisers estimate value using three approaches: market, cost, and income. This process will help you understand how value is professionally estimated, although you won't want to spend the time to become a professional appraiser. A brief description of each method follows.

15

MARKET APPROACH

The market data comparison approach is one of the three standard methods for estimating the value of real estate. The indication of value is based on recent sales of similar properties in the local market. The market approach assumes that the typical buyer views the property as an alternative to buying a different but similar property.

The market approach is most reliable when market activity is normal and there are many close substitutes for the property in the market. When activity is slow, it is difficult to get enough comparable sales for a reliable indication of value. When activity is high, prices may be driven upward to a level that can't be sustained, leading to overstated value. If the subject property is unusual, there may be not be close substitute properties in the market.

To make a market approach estimate, you collect information on recent sales of properties similar to your subject property. These sales are called *comparables*, or "comps" in trade language. The more comps, the better the analysis, but there should be at least three. The sales prices of the comparable properties are adjusted to account for any differences between them and the subject property. Adjustments are commonly made for such features as size, age, condition and quality, date of sale, and location, If special financing was used in the sale, some of the sales price may reflect the benefits of the loan to the buyer, and the price increase due to financing must be separated from the price for the property alone.

Each adjustment is based on a judgment of how much the market is paying for a feature. Adjustments are added or subtracted to make the price of the comparable what it would have been if the property had had the same salient features as the subject property. If the comparable is better than the subject in some regard, its sales price is adjusted down to equate it to the subject. If inferior, the comparable's price is adjusted upward. After all comparables are adjusted, the appraiser estimates market value based on the adjusted sales prices, applying judgment and expertise.

The market approach is often the most useful indication of what the property will likely sell for in the current market. By looking at the way comparables are adjusted, you may learn how certain features are valued in the market. The selection of comparables may indicate how active the market is for properties like the one in which you are interested. If the market is very active, the comparables will be very recent. If not, some of them may be six or more months old. The comparables may also indicate what features are standard in the market.

A key to negotiating the cost of a house is to find comparable sales. An analysis of them will tell you whether you're getting a bargain or overpaying for the house under consideration.

16

COST APPROACH

The cost approach is based on the cost to reproduce the subject property and assumes that the buyer considers the option of new construction when viewing the subject property. The cost approach is generally used as a backup to the market approach, but it may be the primary indication when the property is proposed or new construction or is unique, or when market conditions are abnormal.

The cost approach starts with an estimate of the cost to replace the subject house with up-to-date materials and methods at current costs. This amount is reduced by the estimated depreciation in the appraised property, an adjustment required whenever the house is not brand-new. (Since new buildings have little depreciation, the cost method is often used to appraise new construction.) Depreciation comes in three forms:

1. Physical, or wear and tear from normal use. This may range from faded paint or worn-out carpet to major deterioration in the basic structure of a building.
2. Functional, or a loss in the utility of the property. This may be due to changing tastes or prefer-

ences, such as the introduction of more modern kitchen or bathroom fixtures.

3. External, or a loss in value due to changes outside the property. The opening of a nearby hospital, shopping center or factory or the widening of a street can raise or lower the value of a home.

When the estimated depreciation is subtracted from the replacement cost, the result is an indication of the value of the house alone. The site (land, lot) is valued by comparing it to sites where the most likely use is similar to the subject property. The value of the site is added to the building value to get an indication of property value.

The cost approach also gives an indication of the value of the building and site separately. It may be useful to know how much value is added by the building when a change in use is contemplated. When renovation or modernization is considered, the cost approach may indicate how much value would be added by curing various types of depreciation. Depreciation is considered curable when more value will be added to the property than the cost of correction; it is incurable when the cost of correction exceeds the value added. The analysis may also indicate building features that contribute less to value than they cost. In appraisal terms, these are called *deficiencies* when they are inadequate or obsolete; if too good or expensive for the purpose, they are overimprovements or *superadequacies*.

The cost approach can be a key to negotiating the purchase. If the house is fairly new, find out who built it or get the plans. In either case, get an estimate of the cost of reproduction. If this is less than the owner is asking for essentially the same house, a price reduction is justified. However, be sure that the builder's quote is the full amount, including land and interest during construction.

17

INCOME APPROACH

The income capitalization approach is based on the value of the income produced by the property and assumes that the typical buyer views the property as an investment. The emphasis is on the financial returns from the property rather than on its physical characteristics.

The income approach is seldom used for owner-occupied housing. However, a variation on the technique, called the *gross rent multiplier (GRM)*, can be substituted. Comparable sales are examined in the market for rental houses. Gross rent multipliers—the sales price divided by the monthly gross rent—are calculated for each comparable. A single multiplier or a range is selected to represent the market. This multiplier is then applied to the subject by estimating what the house would rent for and multiplying it by the multiplier. The result is an indication of the property's value.

For example, suppose three homes that were recently sold are now being rented:

A sold for $100,000 and rents for $1,000 monthly (GRM is 100).

B sold for $94,500 and rents for $900 monthly (GRM is 95).
C sold for $84,000 and rents for $800 monthly (GRM is 105).

In each case the selling price is approximately 100 times the monthly rent; so if the property you are considering would rent for $1,000 per month, it is probably worth between $95,000 and $105,000.

The comparables used to estimate the gross rent multiplier should have about the same life expectancies and appreciation potential as the subject property. If not, the indication will not be reliable. In most cases, the value indication is very sensitive to selection of the multiplier. There are many places where owner occupancy is so dominant that this technique cannot be used or would be of limited value. Consequently, don't rely on this technique when deciding how much to offer for a property. Consider the market approach as holding far more validity for a house, while the income approach is the key to valuing an office building or shopping center.

18

AFFORDABILITY AND LOAN QUALIFICATION GUIDELINES

Lending institutions use certain criteria to determine whether you can afford a certain home. More than one criterion may be applied by an institution as a check on both the adequacy of your income and your obligations. To complicate matters, different criteria may be applied by different lenders. Finally, just because a lender says you qualify for a loan doesn't mean that you can easily afford the payments. Stretching your income to its limit means that you'll have nothing left for luxuries or for emergencies.

In the past, qualification rules were relatively simple. You could presumably afford a house priced at 2 to 2.5 times your annual gross income. For example, if your gross income was $40,000 per year, you could afford a house priced up to $100,000. Another qualification guideline was that no more than 25 percent of your gross monthly income nor more than 33 percent of your net income should go toward housing. Because of individual differences in the use of credit and variations in interest rates, loan qualification guidelines have changed.

Current qualification guidelines are more complex than before and depend on the type of loan. Percentages of income that can be spent on housing are shown below.

MAXIMUM RATIO OF PAYMENTS TO GROSS INCOME FOR CONVENTIONAL MORTGAGES

	Fixed-Rate Loan	*Adjustable-Rate Loan*
Loan-to-value to 95%	28%/36%	25%/33%
Loan-to-value to 90%	33%/38%	28%/36%

The first of each pair of percentages is the ratio of housing payments to gross monthly income. Housing payments are defined as principal, interest, taxes, insurance, and condominium fees, but excluding utilities and maintenance. Gross income is the full amount, not reduced by withholding. Your ratio cannot exceed the percentage shown.

You must also pass the second percentage test, total debt payments as a percentage of gross income. Total debt payments are housing debt plus any recurring debt payments of 10 months or more: other real estate, auto, personal charge cards, alimony, and so on.

FHA rules also have two percentage requirements, 38% and 56%, but the definitions are different. First, total housing expenses including utilities and maintenance cannot exceed 38% of net effective income (gross income less federal withholding tax). Second, debt payments cannot exceed 56% of net effective income. Such payments are defined to include expenses for housing, any debt that requires at least 12 months of payments, revolving debt, city and state income taxes, and Social Security payments (FICA withholding).

The Veteran's Administration also has two tests. First, from gross monthly income subtract Social Security withholding, PITI, utilities and maintenance, federal and local withholding, transportation, child support payments, union dues, and all monthly debt payments with six months or more left. The balance of your income must be at least $340 for a one-person household, $570 for two persons, $687 for three, $773 for four; and $803 for five; over five, add $70 for each up to seven. If that balance does not meet the minimum, the prospective borrower will not qualify for the loan. The second test is that all monthly required payments cannot exceed 43% of gross income less Social Security and federal withholding tax.

The chart in the next key and Table 1 in the appendix can be used to determine the principal and interest payments on a loan.

19

MORTGAGE TYPES AND SUITABILITY

The basic type of mortgage that has been prevalent since the 1940s has a fixed interest rate, a fixed payment, and a fixed term and is fully self-amortizing. Other important types include adjustable-rate, graduated-payment, and reverse-annuity mortgages. The term *conventional mortgage* has traditionally referred to a mortgage that is not government guaranteed (by the Veterans Administration) or insured (by the Federal Housing Administration). If you want to make a small down payment, a VA or FHA loan is appropriate if you and the property are both eligible. If ineligible for a government sponsored loan, you may be able to get a conventional loan for up to 95 percent of the property's value, but you must pay for private mortgage insurance.

Fixed-rate mortgages. These loans require equal monthly payments of principal and interest for the life of the loan. The required payment depends on the amount borrowed, term, and interest rate. Sample payments per $1,000 borrowed are as given in the table below. It may take several phone calls and visits to lenders to find the best deal available. While a real estate broker may help, be sure to check rates independently.

Monthly Payments per $1,000 Principal
Amortization Term

Interest Rate	15 Years	20 Years	25 Years	30 Years
8%	9.56	8.36	7.72	7.34
9%	10.14	9.00	8.39	8.05
10%	10.75	9.65	9.09	8.78
11%	11.37	10.32	9.80	9.52
12%	12.00	11.01	10.53	10.29

The most important thing to look for is the *annual percentage rate.* This is the face interest rate, adjusted upward for discount points and other fees and charges. Each *discount point* represents a one-time charge of 1 percent of the mortgage amount. The total amount of points is deducted from the loan amount. Spread over the life of a 30-year loan, each point approximates the equivalent of adding 1/8 percent to the face interest rate. However, the increase is greater for shorter-term loans and for high-rate loans. For example if a loan is repaid after just one year, each point is equivalent to more than a 1-percent rate increase.

In recent years there has been a return to a fast-amortizing fixed-rate loan, notably a 15-year term. Most carry face rates up to 1/2 percent less than their 30-year counterparts. The drawback to the total savings is the increased payment. As the expression goes, it takes money to save money.

A variation on the fixed-rate mortgage is the bi-weekly mortgage. The lender figures the payment on a 30-year monthly payment loan, then requires half to be paid every two weeks. Since there are 26 two-week periods in a year, this is the equivalent of paying 13 months per year. This results in retiring a 30-year loan in 18 to 20 years. The key to its use is your salary income frequency. If you're paid every two weeks, it fits you well. If you're paid monthly, it may not fit well.

Adjustable-rate mortgages (ARMs). These loans usually offer a lower initial rate of interest but carry much uncertainty or risk for the borrower. ARM interest rates are likely to emulate short-term rates, which tend to be volatile. The key to an ARM is being sure that there is a limit on the annual rate change and lifetime change. These limits are called "caps," and a reasonable cap is a 2 percent limit for a one-year change, and a 6 percent limit over the life of a loan. Thus, if your loan begins at 9 percent, it will never exceed 15. Also, be sure that increases in general interest rates above your caps do not extend the loan term. ARMs carry a basic rate plus a margin to result in the actual rate charged. For example, the basic rate may be that of one-year constant-maturity Treasury bills plus a margin of 2 percent, resulting in a fully indexed rate of 11 percent. Suppose the T-bills are 9 percent on an anniversary date—your rate will then be 11 percent for the next year.

A trick some lenders use to make their rates seem competitive is the teaser—an especially low introductory rate. For example, they may offer an ARM with rates calculated as above, but at 7 percent for the first year. If T-bills stay at 9 percent, the lenders have built in an automatic 4 percent rate increase possibly occurring on the first anniversary of the loan. If the rates on T-bills rise, the increase will be even more. A final caution is that the caps may be tied into the fully indexed rate rather than the 7 percent introductory teaser. So a 6 percent lifetime cap is not 13 percent (7 + 6) in this example; rather it could be 17 percent (11 + 6).

Graduated-payment mortgages (GPMs). These loans have fixed interest rates, but the payments start low, then increase by 7.5 percent per year for the first five years. By the sixth year the payment is high enough for full amortization over the next 25 years.

GPMs typically carry an interest rate 1/2 percent higher than that on equivalent fixed-payment loans—a good reason not to get one. However, if you expect your income to rise steadily and can't otherwise afford the payments, a GPM could be for you.

Reverse-annuity mortgages (RAMs). These loans are for mature people who want to use the large equity in their house to supplement their income. They borrow each month from a cooperating lender until a ceiling amount or loan-to-value ratio is reached. The amount borrowed each month, plus interest on the entire loan, is added to the debt. Thus, their equity is diminished rapidly unless the property value appreciates. These loans should not be entered into without legal advice and careful consideration, and under no circumstances should the homeowners place themselves in a situation where they might lose the mortgaged property.

In late 1989, the Department of Housing and Urban Development began an experimental program with Home Equity Conversion Mortgages. If the program proves successful, these loans for elderly will become readily available.

20

THE NEGOTIATING PROCESS

Negotiation is expected in a real estate purchase. The seller sets an offering price, and you know that you can buy the property for that, but your object is to buy it for less. The buyer and seller really need each other, so both benefit by agreement, not disagreement. Sellers are in competition with other sellers and buyers with other buyers, but buyers need sellers and vice versa. The key for both buyer and seller is to have market knowledge of the property value, and to remain open and flexible until an agreement is reached.

Another key is to understand the legal basis of the negotiations and the contract. A contract is reached when there is an offer and acceptance. The contract describes the terms and conditions of purchase. If you are not happy with a contract that has been offered to you, don't sign it expecting to change it later. Once you have signed, the deal is on—unless all parties agree to a change.

When an offer is presented, say from a prospective

buyer to an owner, the owner may reject it outright. Alternatively, the owner may change one or more elements and sign it as amended, then return it to the prospective buyer. This is called a *counteroffer* and is the same as a rejection of the offer with a substitution of a new offer. The smallest change in one provision constitutes a complete rejection of the entire offer. The counteroffer is made by the owner to the prospective buyer, who may, in turn, accept, reject, or counter. A key to negotiations is to realize when to stop negotiating, either by accepting an offer, if adequate, or by breaking off communications when you feel agreement is not possible at the price and terms you want.

Many contract forms have a provision that the offeree (the one who receives the offer) has a certain period of time (for example, until midnight on the second day) to accept the offer or it expires automatically. However, the offer may be withdrawn by the offerer anytime before it is accepted. If an offer has been accepted and the acceptance is en route back to the offerer, it is generally too late for the offerer to back out. It is therefore wise to set a deadline for notifying the offerer, or at least attempted notification before the expiration time passes.

A broker is usually much involved in the negotiation phase. Many people feel more comfortable dealing through a broker rather than face to face with the other party. Many times the broker's commission is earned in this process, as he or she brings buyer and seller to an agreement. In some locales the brokerage commission becomes part of the negotiations. A broker may actually lose compensation, as when the principals look to the broker to close the gap in price difference by surrendering part of the commission. For most brokers, although the commission rate is negotiable, the degree of compromise is limited.

21

PURCHASE CONTRACT PROVISIONS

An offer to buy a house is usually submitted by a prospective buyer using a contract form. In many states, especially in the Northeast, a *binder* is used as the offer to purchase. When the binder has been accepted by both parties, they actually agree to prepare a lengthier *contract of sale* within a few days. The seller's attorney is often assigned this function. By contrast, in the South and West a printed contract form often is filled in by the broker and signed by the buyer and/or seller, without the use of a binder or an attorney.

In real estate anything not in writing doesn't count. If the other party cries "trust me to do that, we don't need to put it in writing," it is all the more reason to be certain it is written in the contract. In the words of the legendary Sam Goldwyn, "A verbal contract isn't worth the paper it is written on."

In some states a certain printed contract form is

mandated for use by all brokers and salesmen, and they must have an attorney draw up the contract if they don't use the mandated form. Office supply stores often have these printed forms for sale at very reasonable prices. The best advice is to consult your own attorney, but if you're determined not to, read carefully, be sure you understand all of the provisions, and do your best to make sure that the other party is trustworthy. There are two types of mistakes: submitting a bad contract and not submitting a good one. Submitting a bad one is far more dangerous. If you're going to err, do it on the safe side.

Common clauses in a contract pertain to:

Parties. Names of buyer(s) and seller(s).

Property. Address (lot and block, city and county, street number) and a statement that all improvements are included. This clause could list items such as draperies, shutters, air conditioners, shrubs, etc.

Purchase price. How much is offered for the property, including cash and mortgages.

Financing terms. How you will pay the seller. This must describe any proposed loan from the seller and any required loans from third parties. Specify the maximum acceptable interest rate so that if rates rise quickly you don't have to buy. Specify the loan type (FHA, VA, or conventional) and other elements you require: adjustable rate, graduated payment, or level payment, and maximum points that you will pay.

Earnest, escrow, hand or good-faith money. This will show the seriousness of your offer and will be forfeited if, after the contract is signed by you and the owner, you fail to close the deal. With a properly worded contingency clause, you will be entitled to a refund of this money if the deal falls through because of the specified contingency.

The amount varies from place to place. In some communities $1,000 is sufficient regardless of the property, whereas 10 percent of the purchase price or more is customary in other areas. Earnest money is deposited in a broker's escrow account, separate from the broker's own money, pending consummation of the sale.

Closing. Buyer and seller must agree on when and where the closing is to take place, which party selects the closing agent, and who pays closing agent fees. Often the buyer dictates when to close.

Title. What type of title insurance or abstract must be provided, and who pays. Lenders will demand a policy for at least the loan balance. You can buy additional title insurance to cover your equity for a one-time payment of a relatively small amount. The type of deed can be important. A general warranty deed is the best type to get, although others may be satisfactory if there are assurances of validity from your lawyer or title company.

Assessments. Who pays for assessments, when they are a lien.

Expiration. Date and time when the offer must be accepted before it becomes void.

Deposit increase. Conditions under which you must increase the earnest money before closing to maintain the contract. For example, if your purchase is contingent on the sale of your old home, the seller may want periodic deposit increases to confirm your sincerity.

Commissions. Which party owes a brokerage commission, to which broker, and the percentage rate or dollar amount.

Pest control inspections. Gives you the right to hire an inspector for insects, and provides other rights or options to buy or repair if wood-destroying insects are found.

Property condition inspections. A typical clause gives you and your representative the right to inspect for electrical, mechanical, plumbing, and structural integrity. If up to a certain dollar value of defects is found (say $1,000), the seller must repair. But if repair costs exceed that, the seller need not close the sale and you need not buy. Without the clause, you may be buying "as is."

Flood plain. It should be specified whether or not the property is in a flood-prone area. In most metropolitan areas a lender will require flood insurance if the house is in the 100-year flood plain.

Sale of other property. Terms of cooperation with buyer if you must sell another property before buying this one.

Contingency release. If you must sell other property before buying, the seller will generally specify the terms of releasing your rights to this contract, such as when another buyer is found for the property under contract.

Prorations. Calls for taxes, interest, insurance, rents, and other items to be prorated between buyer and seller.

Title examination. Allows the buyer (or attorney) to examine title and submit any objections to be cleared prior to closing.

Encumbrances. Buyer is to take title subject to encumbrances, or provide, within a brief time period, objections to restrictions, easements, and unpaid taxes that must be cleared by seller.

Notices. Refers to addresses to which the parties deliver any written instructions pertaining to the contract.

Default. Describes rights if a party defaults. If the buyer defaults, the seller often keeps the earnest money and may be able to collect additional amounts for any damages sustained. In many cases, liquidated damages are provided in the contract, and the buyer must pay them and brokerage commissions. Attorney's fees may also be paid by a defaulting buyer if a court so orders.

Physical possession. Usually allowed to buyer upon title transfer, or perhaps a few days thereafter.

Time. Usually provides that *time is of the essence,* which prohibits delaying tactics of a party.

Signatures. Places for seller(s), buyer(s), and broker to sign.

Other Provisions. This space is for either party to write in any provision or contingency that should be in writing.

22

KEY NEGOTIATING POINTS

Virtually everything in a property transaction is negotiable. This includes:

- The price
- How it is to be paid (all cash at closing, deferred payments, trading other property)
- Who pays closing costs (either party may pay loan discount points, attorney fees, recording costs, title policy premium, property condition inspections, brokerage commission)
- Terms of financing, if the seller provides the loan (amount, interest rate, term of loan)
- Timing of closing (you might set the closing at a date when the money is available)
- Date of possession (you might set this up on closing or shortly thereafter to give the seller a few days to pack up). A lease should be prepared to cover any tenancy.
- Contingencies (sale subject to financing or sale of another property)

The asking price of a house generally leaves room for bargaining. In some areas of the country, the asking price or listed price may exceed what the owner can expect by as much as 10 percent. Realtors believe that the ability to price a house correctly is a sign of professionalism, so in many places the expected selling price is very near the listed price. Information provided by the "Sold" book of multiple listing services and professional advice is quite helpful.

The overall transaction is what counts, not merely the stated price. If you are willing to meet the seller's price, you may be able to get concessions on other items that may be more important. For example, the seller may be willing to finance the sale by lending a substantial amount of the cost. The interest rate and repayment terms then become crucial issues. Getting a lower interest rate on a long-term loan, if only 1 percent lower, can be equivalent to a property price reduction of up to 10 percent.

When negotiating, you shouldn't feel that you are trying to take advantage of the other party. Recognize that offers contain margins for bargaining and that your objective is to get the best deal possible. At the same time, you must be realistic in your demands and be willing to compromise if you really want to close the deal.

A bargaining tactic often seen is the reported presence of another party. The seller or broker may tell you that others have made offers and that yours must be better if you are to land the house. In most instances the report is true or partly true. Still, if you need time yourself to make a decision, don't be hasty. There are two kinds of mistakes: buying the wrong house and not buying the right house. Buying the wrong house is the worse mistake and must be avoided.

23

HOW TO ARRANGE FINANCING

If you've been waiting for interest rates to 'bottom out' before buying, you know how difficult that can be. When rates are falling, there's a temptation to wait for a further decline before buying. But then rates can turn up sharply, and the opportunity may slip away. On the other hand, if you buy, and then interest rates drop even further, you may have an opportunity to refinance, that is, replace your old mortgage with a new one at a better rate.

Whether it is the original mortgage or a refinancing, shop carefully for the best mortgage you can get. A real estate broker can be helpful, but plan to spend several hours on the phone asking for rates. Some newspapers print mortgage rates offered by local lenders once a week. That, too, is useful information, but be sure to call and verify. Take out the Yellow Pages and call as many lenders as you can. Ask for rates, points, and all other costs for the type of loan you want. Decide whether you want FHA, VA, or conventional; a fixed-rate or an ARM; how much down payment you can make; how long you want the term of the loan to be. Organize a tablet with each lender's name, phone number, loan officer, rate, points, fees, lock-in period, and application fees.

Rates have a way of changing quickly, so ask the length of the amount of lock-in (the period that the rate quote will be valid) and amount of the application fee. Some lenders will offer a 60-day lock-in but may want a 1 percent nonrefundable fee. Others will refuse to lock in, especially when rates are volatile, giving you the prevailing rate at closing. Beware of the lender with the lowest quote and a long lock-in. There are unscrupulous lenders who offer a deal that is too good to be true. When closing time comes, they weasel out of the commitment and quote a much higher rate. At that point, you're told to "take it or leave it." Since you have probably made arrangements to move your residence, and it's too late to find another lender, you're in a squeeze and must close that loan at the higher rate. Even some seemingly reputable lenders drag their feet in processing an application when they don't want to honor a commitment because interest rates have suddenly turned up.

Types of lending institutions. Most mortgage loans are sold to investors after they are originated. Often even the right to service the loan (collect payments for a fee) is sold, too. Consequently, it often doesn't matter who the original lender is—you may be dealing with someone else before you make your first payment.

The most common lender for conventional loans and (conventional-insured loans) is a *savings and loan association.* There are more than 3,000 across the United States, and many make home lending their main business. However, the great importance of S&Ls to home mortgage lending has been declining. *Mutual savings banks* are similar in lending patterns, with most concentrated in the Northeast. *Mortgage bankers* also originate loans, but they sell all of them as soon as is practical. They are usually able to offer FHA and VA loans at highly competitive rates, and they process applications quickly. *Commercial banks* also make home mortgages, but traditionally they have not focused their effort in the home mortgage area. They may offer the best rate for the type of loan you seek.

Income requirements and other guidelines for various types of home loans are described in Key 18 on affordability. Some lenders will prequalify you, that is, tell you how much you can borrow. This can give you confidence when shopping for a house, knowing that you can close, and will also expedite the closing time. However, most lenders won't take you seriously until you show them a signed contract.

When you approach a lender, have all your financial papers in order. Make a list of your accounts: checking, savings, credit cards, etc. Include account numbers and balances. Bring copies of car titles. Bring a list of securities you own and their value. Bring copies of 1099 tax forms to show dividend, interest, and royalty income. If you own rental property, bring something to prove you get rental income. If either spouse is divorced, show proof of alimony and/or child care support, whether paying or receiving. List your jobs for the past ten years, addresses, phone numbers, income, and supervisors. Bring your W-2 forms for the past two years. If you've been self-employed, bring tax returns for the past three years. Your lender will want a copy of the sales contract, too.

Help the lender to verify all the items noted above, as this will expedite the loan process. The lender will want money for a property appraisal (about $200-$300) and credit check ($50). In addition, there may be an application fee or lock-in fee, which might be 1 percent of the loan. Ask your lender how long the process normally takes. Call back regularly to be certain there are no unusual snags. Your seller and broker will also appreciate being kept informed of your loan approval status.

Use the Financing Checklist beginning on page 146 to aid your search for the best financing terms. More detailed information on arranging a home loan is available in another Barron's book in this series, *Keys to Mortgage Financing and Refinancing.*

24

DOWN PAYMENT

There are advantages to making a large down payment. The more cash you put up, the less you borrow and the smaller your monthly payments. As a general rule, too, the larger the down payment, the better the mortgage loan terms, but the difference in interest rates might not be significant. With a down payment of 20 percent or more, you don't have to buy private mortgage insurance, saving approximately 2 percent of the amount borrowed at origination, plus one-quarter of 1 percent annually for 10 years. A lower mortgage means there'll be less stress on the household budget.

For some people, however, a smaller down payment is better. Some buyers may not have the extra cash, and others may want to keep a cash reserve for unexpected expenses, household purchases, or investments. The amount of tax-deductible interest expense is greater with a large mortgage, and money not used for the down payment can be invested, even in tax-free municipal bonds.

Typically, a mortgage is the least expensive kind of long-term loan you can get in terms of both interest rate and repayment terms. Also, it is possibly the only type of consumer debt that helps expand one's credit limit. Therefore, if you have limited cash for a down payment, you should take full advantage of the mortgage loan available—as long as you can afford the monthly payments. You may need to get mortgage insurance, which will add to your costs.

Generally, if you have bought what you expect to be your "last house," it's a good policy to make a large down payment, pay the loan off rapidly, and look forward to the day you can burn the mortgage. However, if you are transient, perhaps being transferred around the country by your employer on a regular basis, make a small down payment. That way your money is not tied up in your house.

25

PHYSICAL INSPECTIONS

Your contract should include the right to inspect the property (see Key 21). It is best to get a professional to do this job. If in your own inspections you've noticed anything that looks problematical, jot it down and lend your notes on it to the inspector. Try to be present at the inspection (why should anyone object?) and follow the inspector through the house. You may learn much about the house in a short time, and the inspector may appreciate someone to talk with or help carry a tool.

The inspector may have a checklist to make sure of commenting on the adequacy (typical, marginal, or unsatisfactory) and condition of various items. Objective tests, such as using a thermometer to verify oven temperature readings or a gauge to measure water pressure, should be used wherever possible. These are some things to check:

Appliances. Range, oven, dishwasher, refrigerator (if any), disposal, range-hood, compactor, microwave, intercom, smoke detector.

Plumbing. Pipes, sinks, lavatories, tubs, showers,

commodes, outside faucets, hot water heaters, and sprinkler systems.

Fireplace. Starter, damper, firebox, lintel (face brick), chimney cap.

Heating. Type (oil, gas, electric), furnace capacity, blowers, control thermostat, pilot lights, humidifier.

Air conditioning. Type (electric, gas), compressor capacity, evaporator coil and fan, condensation drain(s).

Electrical. Circuit breaker or fuse adequacy, outlets, light fixtures, ceiling fans, garage door openers, doorbell, bathroom equipment. If you expect to install heavy appliances such as a dishwasher or air conditioner, you must have wiring that can carry heavy loads.

Foundation. Type, condition, water drainage.

Roof. Type (wood shingle, composition), condition, ventilation, insulation (type and R value), flashing.

Structure. Load-bearing walls, ceilings, floors.

Floor and wall coverings. The inspector may note defects or repairs needed in linoleum and carpet. However, your expectations of an inspector must be reasonable—the inspector may not find problems that are well hidden, such as a carpet stain that is underneath heavy furniture.

Wood-destroying insects. A qualified pest control inspector is needed to assure freedom from wood-destroying insects. Termites are the most feared, but powderpost beetles and old house borers can be damaging. Carpenter ants are common but don't necessarily cause structural damage.

Contaminants. Environmental concerns are an increasing problem. Radon (which is a naturally occurring form of radioactivity) can be a severe problem, especially in tightly sealed houses. The ground and groundwater could be contaminated by pollutants released by nearby factories, landfills, and so on. Properties that have been used for agricultural purposes and golf courses are suspect. All present and previous owners may be responsible for clean-up—that is, if you can find them. You might not want to buy any property that has a severe contamination problem, so make it a point to discover the history of land use for your proposed purchase.

Dollarize. The estimated repair cost of each item can be noted for presentation to the owner. If everyone is fortunate, they will be minimal. Should the house need extensive repairs, recheck purchase contract provisions and negotiate from there.

26

THE CLOSING
(SETTLEMENT)

Closing, also called *settlement* in some parts of the country, is the point at which money and property change hands. Conditions of the sales contract are to be fulfilled at that moment. You will sit across a table from the seller. In effect, you will hand over a check to the seller and receive a deed in exchange. However, the reality is that your lenders (or representative) will be present to file the mortgage loan you are borrowing. There is likely to be a lawyer or other title company representative present to account for the transaction: money and documents. In many states closing is accomplished through an escrow agent— buyer and seller can sign documents and exchange money through this trusted third party, without the necessity for both to be present at the same time or even on the same day. The lender (or escrow agent) makes certain that documents are recorded and money disbursed properly.

Under the Real Estate Settlement Procedures Act (RESPA) you have certain rights. These are described in a booklet, *Settlement Costs and You*, which every lender must give each potential borrower soon after a loan application is requested. One right is to inspect the settlement papers before closing, with whatever figures are then available. Look at the figures the day before closing so you can deal with any problems before the actual closing.

The settlement form can be intimidating unless you know what to look for. First, check the charges to the buyer (debits) and be certain that every one is valid. Don't be afraid to ask. Then look for credits to the buyer. Make certain that everything you're using to pay for the property is there. For example, if property taxes are due at the end of the year, the seller owes you for taxes until the time of closing. If the seller will remain for five days after closing, charge rent for those five days. If the seller has not finished repairs that are required by the contract, there had better be an adjustment at closing or you should get a check. Report anything that might be wrong with the proposed papers. Computers can make a change and print out revised papers in seconds. By reviewing the papers the day before closing you will also see how much cash you will need. Many lenders require a certified check or cashier's check. Learning what you need in advance will avoid snags at closing.

Discount points paid on a mortgage to purchase your principal residence are deductible if such charges are an established practice in the area and the amount is within what is generally charged. Make sure that discount points are labeled as such in the settlement papers, and pay for them with a separate check to show the IRS that you specifically paid them. If the seller has agreed to pay discount points, you will get no deduction. Neither will the sellers, because it is not their debt, though they can deduct such payments from their taxable gain on the sale. Consequently, it is better for you to pay points and negotiate a lower purchase price than it is for you to pay more for the house and have the seller pay points. Other fees for services involved in closing are not deductible.

Money for hazard insurance and taxes must be paid at closing. Lenders typically require you to purchase at least 14 months of insurance (paying the first year's policy in full and getting two months ahead of the next year), and deposit at least two months of taxes in advance, in addition to prorated amounts.

Title insurance is paid only once. Your lender will insist on it to the extent of the loan amount. You can buy a policy to cover your equity, at a modest fee. Some people feel it is unnecessary, while others who know of horror stories in title problems will urge you to get it.

The closing costs a buyer will likely incur, some of which the seller may agree to pay, include fees for:

Title insurance
Escrow
Legal assistance
Survey
Loan origination
Appraisal report
Credit check
Notary
Recording
Inspections

27

KEEPING RECORDS

For tax, insurance, financial, and legal reasons, it's important to keep good records on your house, especially records concerning its purchase and ownership. These include receipts for money paid on or before the closing, a copy of the mortgage note or deed of trust, your copy of the deed, your warranties on the house, and any FHA- or VA-related documents.

Insurance records should include a copy of the hazard or homeowner's insurance policy; mortgage, life, or flood insurance policies; and a list of your personal property in the home and its value. Keep records of money spent on maintenance, repairs, and especially home improvements. Photographs of your home and its contents, including closets, will be invaluable when it comes to proving losses for insurance purposes.

In a tax dispute with the IRS, the burden of proof is on the taxpayer. You need to keep the records required to prove your tax basis for your home—that is, the point from which gains, losses, and, if leased, depreciation are computed—and perhaps for all the homes you have previously owned.

A good precaution is to put all important papers and photographs in a bank vault. That way they exist even if a catastrophe hits your home. You might wish to keep photocopies at home for convenient reference.

It is a good idea to keep a list of valuable records and their location, and tell your attorney. In the event that anything should happen to you, others will know where to find the important papers.

A sample list of items that affect your tax basis is below:

Purchase items found on closing statements:

Purchase price	Title search
Appraisal fees	Title insurance
Attorney's fees	Survey
Recording fees	

Improvements that are added to basis (repairs and maintenance on a personal residence are not tax deductible nor can they be added to basis):

Air conditioning	Driveway paving
Attic flooring, finishing	Electrical outlets
Alarm	Exhaust fans
Basement improvements	Fences
Basketball goal	Fireplace
Bathtub	Fixtures
Boiler	Flooring
Built-in bookcase(s)	Furnace
Cabinets	Fuses
Carpeting	Garage
Chimney	Garage door opener
Circuit breakers	Garden
Countertops	Gates
Curtains	Grading
Deck	Greenhouse
Dishwasher	Gutters
Drainpipes	Heat pump
Drapes	Hot water heater

Insulation	Security system
Intercom	Shelves
Kitchen appliances	Shutters
Landscaping	Shrubs
Lawn sprinkler	Sidewalks
Linoleum	Skylights
Locks	Sinks
Mailbox	Stairs
Medicine chest	Storm doors
Mirrors	Survey
Paneling	Swimming pool
Patio	Telephone outlets
Plumbing	Television antenna
Porch	Tile
Radiators	Trees
Railings	Vanity
Roofing	Venetian blinds
Screens	Wall coverings

Items that are subtracted from the selling price to determine the gain include:

Advertising expenses	Legal expenses
Brokerage commission	Loan prepayment fee
Discount points	Title policy

28

SALE OR RENTAL OF HOUSE

Selling. You may need to sell your present house to get the cash for a new one. Also, you might think about what life would be like with two house payments and decide that one payment is plenty. If so, put a contingency clause in the contract to buy, so that you can't be forced to buy unless you've sold your old home. Some sellers will accept that; others will counter with a 48-hour notice to terminate your contract. That is, if another buyer decides to buy the house that you want, the owner tells you that you have 48 hours to decide whether to delete the contingency and set a closing date or to release the contract. If you really can't handle two payments, you'd better let it go.

Conservative people consider the sale of their house the very first step to buying another. They won't even look for another place until the check for the sale is in the bank. This means they will have the trouble of finding temporary quarters and moving again when they find a permanent home. How you handle the sale of your old home is your decision.

Renting out your former home. Renting may be a good choice in a number of circumstances. You might have a temporary job assignment in another city but expect to return after a year or so; or you might be eager to move up to a better house even though you do not find a buyer for your old home. Also, you might want to move now but keep the old home for retirement. Finally, you might want to retain your old home as an investment.

By renting your home instead of selling, you receive income to offset mortgage payments and the costs of upkeep. You also can take advantage of depreciation tax deductions and enjoy holding your property while it appreciates in value. But renting your home does alter your tax benefits as a homeowner; so consult your tax advisor before renting.

If you do rent it, interview your tenants carefully. Make certain they'll be compatible with your house. Get a security deposit and an additional pet deposit— that is, if you allow a pet. Use a good lease, one that is complete, firm, and fair. Sometimes a stationery or office supply store can provide a preprinted residential lease, though you might ask a broker or join the local apartment association.

Comply with your duties under the lease and make every possible effort to determine that your tenants also comply. If they are in violation, act quickly and firmly. Most successful landlords keep the relationship on a strictly business basis. Don't let the tenant be late with rent because he or she has a charming personality.

Be mindful of income tax consequences if you rent your old house. On rental property you can deduct interest, taxes, and all necessary and reasonable expenses. However, if you are in your new house for two years and haven't sold the old one, the tax on the gain from the old one will be triggered when it is eventually sold. This can be a substantial amount.

29

ENERGY CONSERVATION

Insulation needs. You can reduce heat loss or gain in your home by adding insulation. But do you need it? That depends on whether the reduction in your utility bill is large enough to offset the cost of added insulation.

The first layer of insulation may do a lot to reduce heat flow, and additional insulation may not be justifiable. Insulation is purchased by its R, or resistance, value. The greater the resistance to heat transfer, the larger the R value. In a temperate climate, values of R-11 in walls, R-19 in ceilings, and R-26 to R-30 in attics are recommended, but these vary for each region.

In general, if the wall contains some insulation, it's not advisable to attempt to apply more. Before you decide to add insulation, check to see what's already in your home.

Heating costs. Some keys to lowering winter heating bills are:

1. Set your thermostat at 68° F. or lower in the

daytime and at 55° F. or lower during the night. If you feel chilly at these temperatures, try wearing warmer clothes and using more bed covers. It's cheaper than paying for the extra fuel needed to keep you comfortable in a short-sleeved shirt.

2. Have your furnace inspected, cleaned, and adjusted regularly, and make sure you clean or replace the filters about once every 30 days. Dirty filters make your heater work harder and use more energy.

3. Make sure your vents or radiators aren't blocked by furniture or draperies. You want to get all the warm air you're paying for.

Hot water conservation. There are five steps you can take to reduce your costs for hot water:

1. Repair your leaky faucets. A leak of one drop per second can waste more than 50 gallons of heated water each month.

2. Turn down your thermostat. Water at 120° F. or lower may be adequate for the needs of your household.

3. Insulate your hot water tank and pipes.

4. If you have plenty of water pressure in your hot water system, you may want to install flow restrictors. A flow restrictor can substantially reduce the amount of water you use for your morning shower.

5. Keep your hot water tank clean by draining it once a year.

Air leaks. Most air leaks from the home through windows, electrical outlets, air conditioner ducts, and joints between walls and floors.

Examine your doors and windows to see if weather stripping should be replaced. Check the duct system from the furnace to each room outlet. Usually, leakage occurs at the furnace connection and at the outlets. Hold a piece of lightweight tissue near areas thought to be leaking. If the tissue moves, seal the area.

Construction mistakes. A house may come with built-in energy wasters. It is worthwhile to check the cost of repairing or replacing these.

1. Oversizing of heating and cooling equipment— that is, furnaces and air conditioners that are too big. Oversized equipment costs more to purchase and operate and gives less comfort than properly sized equipment.
2. Inadequate attention to air leaks.
3. Inadequately insulated heating and cooling pipes or ducts in unconditioned spaces.
4. Inadequately insulated basements.
5. Glassed areas installed without concern for heat gain in warm sunshine and heat loss on winter nights. In most circumstances, the major glass areas of your house should face south. Such an exposure is generally the most pleasant and energy-efficient. In winter, a southern exposure allows your front windows to receive bright, warm sunshine all day, while the back of the house is turned toward the cold north winds. As the sun climbs higher in summer, trees or awnings can shade your southern windows, while only the smaller eastern and western exposures of the house will receive the direct morning and afternoon sunshine.

30

INCOME TAX DEDUCTIONS

Generous tax deductions are provided homeowners for real estate taxes and mortgage interest. Each dollar of deduction is worth some percentage—presently up to 33 percent in federal tax savings—which provides a substantial reduction in one's after-tax housing cost. Deductions are allowed in the year paid, but prepayment does not provide a deduction. For example, suppose you pay $800 monthly for principal and interest and $200 for taxes and insurance; the latter amount goes into escrow. Of the $200, your deductible amount is whatever your lender disbursed to the taxing authorities during the year. And, of course, the interest portion of your mortgage payment is tax deductible—it is received by the lender. Principal payments are never deductible.

At one time, interest deductions were virtually unrestricted and unlimited, but now there are some restrictions. At purchase you may incur discount points, which may be deductible as described in Key 26.

Interest on up to $1 million of indebtedness to acquire, build, or substantially improve a residence is deductible as acquisition debt. The interest on home equity loans up to $100,000 is deductible, no matter what the money is used for, provided total loans don't exceed the property's fair market value. If a mortgage is refinanced, the new loan is considered acquisition debt to the amount of the remaining balance on the old loan. If more was borrowed in refinancing than owed previously, the excess is considered an equity loan, subject to the $100,000 limit. A few other observations are:

1. Up to two residences may be used for acquisition and home equity loans. A boat or mobile home qualifies provided it has living accommodations including cooking, toilet, and sleeping facilities.
2. The residence(s) is recorded security for the loans.
3. Amounts not deductible as housing interest are considered personal interest. Ten percent of personal interest is deductible in 1990, none thereafter.
4. Limits on debt are halved for married people filing separate returns.
5. Home mortgages placed before October 13, 1987, are grandfathered, even those that exceed these limits.

31

HOME OFFICE

If you use your home for business, certain tax deductions may be allowed, but the rules are stringent. The home office must be used *regularly* and *exclusively* as a principal place of business or as a place to meet customers, patients, or clients if that is part of your business. If your office room is used for a part of the time as a recreational, television, or guest room, it will not qualify. Just using your office to pursue investments won't qualify the room.

If you are employed, your home office must be for the convenience of your employers or there is no deduction. You'll have great difficulty showing that an office is for your employers' convenience if they provide you with some type of office—your home office is probably for your convenience in that situation. But you could have another business. For example, let's say that you teach school during the day and sell cosmetics at night. The spare bedroom or den that you use as an office, where you maintain inventory and have a telephone, could qualify because it is your principal place of business for cosmetics—even though teaching earns you more money. However,

86

you must not carry out any other activities in that part of the house.

Let's suppose that you pass the tests for a home office deduction; the deduction may still be limited. You cannot use a home office deduction to generate a tax loss. And certain rules must be followed in a certain order. First, begin with gross income and subtract direct expenses, such as inventory sold, an answering machine, and bookkeeping help. Then subtract office expenses in this order: interest and taxes, operating expenses and depreciation. If the result is a loss, it may not be used to offset other income—but the loss may carry forward to years in which you have business income.

For example, suppose you sold $15,000 worth of cosmetics and incurred an $8000 inventory cost, plus $500 for telephone expenses (a second line to your house was used). The difference is $6500. Suppose further that interest and taxes allocated to your home office, based on square footage of floor space, were $4000. That leaves $2500. Operating expenses (utilities were $1000) and depreciation are $2000. The result would be a $500 loss. However, losses are prohibited, so the loss can only be used in a future year when you have taxable income from the business.

If the business takes in little, your deduction will be limited. Keep in mind that you can always deduct interest and taxes as an itemized deduction rather than as a home office expense.

The home office deduction for the self-employed belongs on Schedule C of Form 1040. If you're not self-employed, put the deduction on Schedule A of 1040, with Form 2106 attached. The deduction for employees is subject to a 2 percent floor.

That schedule asks the question: "Are you deducting expenses for an office or business in your home?" Naturally, you must answer the question honestly. Some observers believe that a Yes answer will trigger an audit unless the home office is your sole place of business. Most accountants agree that if you rightfully can claim the home office deduction, you should do so. The law allows it provided you meet the stringent requirements.

You might need to sell your home after claiming a home office deduction. If so, its basis will have been reduced by the depreciation, and that portion of the gain is taxable, triggered by the sale, no matter how much your next house costs. A way to avoid triggering the gain is by converting the office back to residential use for the year of the sale.

32

INSURANCE REQUIREMENTS

Most mortgage lenders will require you to carry hazard insurance to at least the amount of the mortgage. You can carry more, generally to the cost of replacing your home or its market value. Hazard insurance protects against such casualties as fire and other damage caused by the elements (but not flooding from a nearby rising creek). A homeowner's policy, which also offers protection against theft, is commonly used. Ask your agent to sit down with you and explain the various types of coverage.

Some policies are standardized: HO-1 offers basic protection; HO-2 adds protection for certain items such as burst water pipes; HO-3 is "all-risk" coverage (but still excludes floods, earthquakes, war); HO-4 is a renter's policy; HO-6 is for condos or co-ops; and HO-8 is for older homes.

The *deductible* (what you pay for each loss) is an important component of the rate. Rates are reduced as deductibles increase. The *co-insurance clause* specifies what minimum percentage of value must be insured for before the insurer will cover a loss in full. In no case will the insurer pay more than the total policy amount, however. Ask your agent about hazards covered by different policies and he'll probably show a picture book of coverage: glass breakage, hail damage, wind damage, etc. *Replacement cost coverage* is often available at extra cost if you want to recover the full value—otherwise depreciation is subtracted from the reimbursement.

Personal property coverage is included to some extent in the typical homeowner's policy, often to 50 percent of the insured amount of your house. So if you carry $100,000 on your house, you may automatically have $50,000 on its contents. But personal property insurance covers only ordinary household belongings. Insurance on expensive art, jewelry, or sterling silver must be "scheduled" (meaning that you pay extra) and possibly appraised for you to be able to collect above a certain amount—often $200 to $1,000 depending on the item.

Actual cash value is often the standard coverage on contents. For example, if your seven-year-old television is stolen, you may be able to collect only a fraction of its cost, say 30 percent, because it has a ten-year life and was seven years old when the loss occurred. Thus, you get paid for the three remaining years—or about what it could be sold for. With replacement cost insurance you'll recover enough to replace it new, but you'll pay more for the annual premium.

Take photos, movies, or a videotape of your home's interior, including the insides of closets and drawers. Put the film in a safety deposit box. In the event of a fire or other loss you'll be able to show what you owned. Also, place the insurance policy in a bank vault. Keep a photocopy at home for reference.

Liability insurance. Most homeowner's insurance policies have a provision for liability insurance, often up to $100,000, and at least $1,000 of medical bills. Be sure this protection is adequate for a personal injury. A guest may trip on loose carpet, a pedestrian may fall because you didn't shovel snow, or a child may drown in your swimming pool. Keep your property in the safest possible condition, but carry adequate insurance as well.

Flood insurance. The U.S. Army Corps of Engineers has prepared maps showing flood-prone zones caused by watersheds in metropolitan areas. The maps indicate land in the 100- and 500-year flood plain but do not designate the areas of more frequent flooding. Consequently, if property is in the 100-year flood plain, investigate further to discover the actual estimated flooding frequency.

You may call the Corps of Engineers' regional office for flood plain information about specific locations, but flood plains may change as land is developed.

Most homes in flood-prone areas qualify for national flood insurance. Many lenders will require homeowners to purchase flood insurance as a condition to granting a mortgage loan in a flood-prone area. To determine whether flood insurance is available in your community, contact your insurance agent or the National Flood Insurance Program, Baltimore, MD.

33

PROPERTY TAXES

Determining property taxes. Property taxes are a prime revenue source for counties, cities, and school districts. You may receive a bill from each of these jurisdictions, generally based on an estimated value of your property.

You have the opportunity to provide a statement of your property's estimated value. The assessor may adjust this estimate or make a separate estimate. From this assessed value, exemptions may be deducted, including homestead exemptions and exemptions for the elderly and disabled, if there are provisions in your state law for doing so. Finally, the tax rate is applied to determine the amount of tax due.

Revaluation. Your house will be reassessed periodically for tax purposes. If the tax value of your home is low in relation to that of other properties in the area, a revaluation may lead to an increase in your taxes, so that you may have to make a substantial lump-sum payment when your tax comes due. In addition, your monthly escrow deposit to cover taxes will increase.

Income tax effects. Property taxes are deductible from the federal income tax for those who itemize deductions. Generally, you can deduct taxes paid. However, the amount paid to an escrow account is not relevant—the amount the escrow agent paid that year is what matters in figuring your deduction. When you buy or sell a house, check the closing statement for tax amounts prorated to the other party. You may discover a tax deduction because you reimbursed the other party for taxes he paid or will pay.

Transactions. When you are buying, selling, or donating property, you should not rely on a tax assessor's valuation as a guide to establishing its price or value. Some assessors are conservative in estimating value. Many assessors have so many properties to value in such a short time that their assessments offer only an approximation of market value. Some properties are assessed at less than their full market value for various legal purposes. Finally, assessments may not have been updated for several years.

Questions. If you have questions about your property tax assessment, property tax appraisal records are open to the public. Thus, you can verify the description of your property, including such items as living area, age, exterior construction, and number of bathrooms.

These records also provide information about the depreciation allowance made for the age and condition of the property. After examining these items for your property, you may want to review similar information for other property in the tax district. Such records may help you verify that you have received equal treatment in revaluation.

34

HOMEOWNERS' ASSOCIATIONS

If you buy a unit in a condominium, you automatically become a member of the homeowners' association. The main duty of the association is to oversee the common property, since everything outside your unit and those of your neighbors belongs to all owners in common.

To do this job, the association will generally have a board of directors elected by the owners to make policy decisions and to see that the necessary management tasks are accomplished. Many large condominiums also employ professional management companies to perform daily tasks.

In general, the board is responsible for maintenance of the grounds and common facilities, paying taxes, obtaining liability and hazard insurance, collecting monthly fees from the owners, and enforcing the condominium bylaws. These tasks can become very complex and may require long hours of work by members of the board.

Most condominium associations require owners to

pay a fee, which may vary from $10 to more than $200 per month. This money is used to meet the association's responsibilities for development, management, and upkeep of the common areas. For a major repair, an additional assessment may be necessary. The association must pay for cleaning, lawn care, utilities, repairs, taxes, and insurance. There may also be recreational and social facilities to maintain, such as a pool or clubhouse. The association may employ a professional manager to oversee these duties.

Before buying a condominium, you should read and understand the bylaws, the rules that govern the development. The bylaws are designed to provide the type of atmosphere most owners want, and they are binding on all owners.

Because the declaration and bylaws are often overwhelming in length and may be difficult to comprehend, it's wise to seek professional help in understanding them. A lawyer or management firm that specializes in condominiums should be able to explain what the documents mean. Counsel should be sought before you sign a sales contract, but don't wait until the last minute to seek help. It may take your lawyer several days to interpret the documents, and you'll want to avoid having to make a hasty decision.

These matters also hold, but to a lesser extent, for homeowner associations in single-family or townhouse developments.

35

RENOVATION, REMODELING, REHABILITATION

As a general rule, the cost of a home improvement will be recovered on resale if it brings the property up to standards prevailing in the neighborhood. On the other hand, if the improvement causes the property to become markedly superior to other homes in the neighborhood, you may not recoup its cost on resale.

Keep in mind that cost is not the same as value. Sometimes a low-cost improvement can make a home much more marketable. In other situations, however, an expensive improvement that is considered desirable by a homeowner will have little or no value in the eyes of prospective purchasers.

Adding a room, upgrading windows and floors, and landscaping generally will add more to the value of the house than the cost of the improvement. And a swimming pool may be a good investment if your neighborhood is already dotted with pools. On the other hand, an Olympic-size swimming pool in a cool climate may even detract from the value of a home. The full cost of extravagant remodeling jobs and overimprovements is seldom recovered.

When planning a capital improvement, consider how long you intend to own the home and how the improvement will be viewed in the resale market. Make the improvement only if you expect to recover the cost through a combination of enjoyment and resale price.

Select a home improvement contractor with care. Ask the prospective contractor for a list of recent customers, and call these people to find out if they were satisfied with the work. Ask the Better Business Bureau if any complaints have been filed about the contractor's performance. Get estimates from two or more contractors and compare material to be used, warranty terms, and other factors, as well as price. Cheapest isn't always best.

Before you sign a contract, make sure it contains a detailed description of the work to be performed, and be certain you understand all parts of the contract. Make certain the work has been completed in accordance with the written contract before final payment.

You may need to get a *building permit* for home improvements. You will pay a nominal fee and agree to have the work inspected by an official of the city. The building code describes certain types of materials and design standards that must be used. There are usually separate codes for the structure, plumbing, and electrical and heating systems of your property. For some tasks, you may be required to hire a licensed contractor to comply with the code. In any case, your builders should be familiar with local codes so that their work will be approved.

Arrange a home improvement loan in advance. Bring the lender a written contract that contains an adequate legal description of the property and sets forth the price, the time for payments, and specific descriptions of the planned work.

Be frugal but fair in setting up a payment schedule with the contractor. Beware of those who demand most of the money up front "to buy materials." There are people in the business who take the money, start the job, and then go off to an "emergency" on the other side of town for several weeks. When you control the money, you control the job.

36

REFINANCING

At some point during the ownership of a house it may be worthwhile to refinance. This involves replacing the existing mortgage with a new loan. Refinancing may be used to reduce debt service or to take equity out of a property. Cash from refinancing may be used for other purposes such as educational or medical needs, or to get capital needed to invest or start a business.

Refinancing can be expensive. Taking out new loans requires payment of origination fees, application fees, and discount points. Retiring the old loan may require payment of a prepayment penalty. In some cases, however, when you refinance with the lender who made the original loan, some of the costs are waived. This depends on how far the lender is willing to go in order to keep the loan. Your biggest cost is often discount points on the new loan (tax deductible over the life of the loan; see Key 26). You can reduce your costs by finding a loan with no or few points, and you can reduce your cash outlay by finding a lender who will finance the costs with the new loan.

Reducing your interest rate. Refinancing can be used

to reduce your cost of debt service when interest rates have declined. The new loan is made for the amount of the old loan balance, but with a lower interest rate. The savings in payments must be enough to outweigh the costs of the refinancing. You can calculate the number of months it takes to pay back these outlays by dividing the total costs of refinancing by the monthly difference in payments. The number of months should be less than the time you expect to continue owning the property.

Extracting home equity. You can cash in some of your equity when the value of the property has risen. This is done by refinancing for an amount greater than the old loan. If interest rates are higher than the rate on the old loan, you might consider adding a second mortgage. This lets you keep the old loan and may save money on debt payments.

Improving loan type or terms. Another use of refinancing is to improve the terms on the debt. The existing loan may have a balloon payment due in a few years or it may be an adjustable-rate loan. When long-term, fixed-rate loans are available at reasonable rates, it may be prudent to change over before you are forced to seek new financing.

There are now ceilings on the allowable interest deduction for home acquisition loans ($1 million) and equity loans ($100,000). If you exceed these ceilings, the interest is personal interest. See Key 30 for more detail.

37

USING A BROKER

If you're considering selling your home, you need to decide whether to sell the house yourself or to list it with a broker. Listing does not necessarily mean that you will end up with less money for your house because of the broker's commission. Skilled agents can often negotiate a high price. Before you decide to sell yourself, consider these points.

First, are you in a hurry? If you are, you may become frustrated by your inability to attract prospective buyers quickly. Next, are homes in your area in demand? If so, you are more likely to do well by handling the sale yourself. Do you know where mortgage money is available? If not, you'll need to find out. Do you know what features buyers in your area are seeking? Does your home contain such features? It will be easier to sell if it does. You should weigh all the factors before deciding whether or not to sell your home yourself.

A broker's level of activity in your neighborhood is a good sign of interest, especially if he or she has sold many houses. Ask friends who have recently sold to tell you about their transaction. Which broker did they use? Did your friends receive fair treatment and good results, or are they bitter about some aspect of the transaction? What about pricing and time on the market, selling efforts, showing procedures, and just plain courtesy?

You may interview several brokers before selecting one that you feel will do the best job. Don't make the selection on the basis of who estimates the highest value; it's not uncommon for a broker to give an unrealistic figure just to get the listing, and then to reduce the price in order to sell quickly.

Ask brokers about what is happening in your neighborhood. What has sold and what hasn't? Ask why. Find out about time on the market and other market conditions. Ask brokers how they will advertise *your* house. What media will be used? Will they hold an open house periodically? Do they sell houses in your price range? Do they belong to the multiple listing service? What size is their firm? More important, is the firm a member of a national relocation service or franchise? (This may be a clue as to whether out-of-town buyers will use their services.) On the other hand, a small firm may be able to offset this advantage by offering more individualized service.

Ask how long a listing the broker feels is needed and what commission rate will be charged. If you are vacating the house before selling it, find out about maintenance. Will the broker see that it is properly maintained while you're away? Is there a charge for this?

Give yourself time to evaluate the services offered by the brokers you meet. Feel free to discuss matters with friends and neighbors who have used them before selecting one.

38

LISTING
CONTRACTS

A listing is a written agreement between an owner and a broker. If the broker presents you with a contract to buy your house offered by a ready, willing, and able buyer at the terms in the listing, you are obligated to pay that broker a commission. You can change your mind about selling by not signing the contract of sale, but you'll still owe the broker the full commission.

Main types of listings are:

Open: The listing can be given to another broker.

Exclusive: No other brokers can sell. The owner himself can sell without paying a commission.

Exclusive right to sell: Your broker gets a commission no matter who sells, even if you sell yourself without the broker's help.

Net: The broker's commission is whatever the buyer pays above a set amount.

MLS: Multiple listing service: Typically an exclusive right to sell is given to one broker, who has agreed to share the listing with all other members of the local MLS.

Items to be negotiated in a listing are:

Term. Most brokers want listings for a minimum of 90 days, though anything from 30 to 180 might be acceptable.

Commission. Some brokers will not accept less than 6 percent; others want even more for difficult homes, and some will accept less if the home is expected to sell quickly.

Reservation list. If you tried to sell before you listed and have some prospects, some brokers will respect your list by agreeing not to charge a commission if you sell to someone on your list of prospects.

Lock box. Brokers like to place a 'lock box' on your door to make sure your key is readily accessible to other brokers when you're not home. Some home-owners are concerned about theft by anyone who has access to the lock box. If this is a concern, don't allow the lock box.

For Sale sign. A broker wants to have a 'For Sale' sign on display in your yard. If you don't want such a public advertisement of your house, you need not give sign permission to anyone.

Subsequent contact with prospect. If someone to whom your broker showed the house buys it after the listing expires, do you owe a commission? This may depend on the intent of the parties, how much time has elapsed, state law, and what's written in the contract. In general, it's not a good idea to get involved in such an arrangement, either as a buyer or as a seller.

39

ADVERTISING AND MARKET APPEAL

Whether you are selling your home yourself or working with an agent, here are some suggestions to help you sell your house more quickly.

Curb appeal is important. The lawn should be mowed and edged, the flowerbeds weeded, and the lot kept free of debris. Scrub or paint the front door so that the home looks neat, clean, and inviting.

Windows should be washed and drapes opened to create an impression of airiness and light. If prospects are looking at night, be sure plenty of lights are on.

Rooms should not be crowded with furniture. Give potential buyers the opportunity to imagine how their furnishings would fit in. But don't leave rooms totally bare, either, even if you've already moved.

Buyers are distracted by television, stereos, and noisy children. Give the would-be purchaser a quiet atmosphere in which to view your home.

Any information that may be helpful should be available to prospective buyers. Make information accessible that will answer these commonly asked questions:

- What date are you planning to move?
- Why are you selling?
- How old is the home, and who built it?
- Have you maintained records of utility expenses, maintenance costs, and annual taxes?
- Is the home completely insulated, and with what type of material?
- Do you plan to include draperies, appliances, and other items in the sale?
- Have you made recent improvements or additions, such as a new appliance or a ceiling fan?

Being able to answer these questions promptly is an important step toward promoting the sale of your home.

Running a newspaper ad is important. The ad must convey the most vital information in as few words as possible. Including the proper information helps an ad achieve its major purpose: getting telephone inquiries. If callers have a better idea of whether your house suits their needs, neither they nor you will waste time. Take time to design an effective ad.

40

PRICING AND NEGOTIATING

When you sell a house, carefully check market conditions. If you're in a seller's market, typified by rising prices and few homes on the market, you can deal from strength. Get an estimate of your home's market value, and then add a substantial margin to that to leave room for further appreciation or bargaining. Sometimes an out-of-town buyer may fall right into your lap and pay your asking price.

A buyer's market, on the other hand, is characterized by many houses for sale with little activity and prices headed downward. You may have to undercut the competition if you really want to sell, possibly by a significant amount if you want to sell quickly (although a quick sale of real estate occurs infrequently). No matter how low you set the price, you still need a buyer to make an offer.

There are two sources available for help in estimating your home's value. An appraisal by a professional appraiser represents an impartial and expert opinion of the property's value. Many experts in the field are members of a professional organization. Some leading ones, with designations in parentheses, are:

Society of Real Estate Appraisers (SREA, SRPA, SRA)

American Institute of Real Estate Appraisers (MAI, RM)

National Society of Real Estate Appraisers (RA, CRA, MREA)

American Society of Appraisers (ASA, FASA)

National Association of Independent Fee Appraisers (IFA)

A real estate broker can help you by performing a "comparative market analysis," which is based on the broker's experience and knowledge of the local market. However, qualifications and lack of independence from the transaction render the broker's estimate less objective.

Your individual situation has much to do with pricing and negotiating. Are you desperate to sell? If you've lost your job or moved away, you may be in this situation. Instead, you might be just anxious. Although you must sell, you can hold on for a lengthy period. Some sellers are "proud." They don't really need to sell and can wait for the right offer. They put their house on the market to show, hoping for a high price.

While pricing isn't everything, the more competitive your price, the more likely you are to sell quickly. Other negotiating items are discussed in Key 22. The bottom line is that you must be flexible if you really want to sell, and be prepared to compromise.

While everything is negotiable, monetary items most likely to be negotiated are:

1. Loan discount points
2. Loan origination fees
3. Other closing costs
4. Amount of earnest money
5. Repairs or improvements
6. Seller financing terms
7. Brokerage fee

Nonmonetary items include:

1. Closing date
2. Moving date
3. Conditions (subject to financing, sale of other house)
4. Required inspections
5. Warranties

41

FINANCING A SALE

When selling a property, you may assist a buyer by providing some or all of the financing needed. In some cases a small second mortgage may be extended, but when bank loans are not available, you, the seller, may have to consider providing the bulk of the purchase price by accepting a mortgage for nearly the full price.

The major terms and considerations of typical seller financing are:

- **Length of mortgage.** Since you probably do not want to wait 25 or 30 years for the money and the buyer wants to avoid the high monthly payment associated with a short-term loan, a *balloon mortgage* may be used. Monthly payments can be based on a 25-year amortization schedule, but the entire loan matures (balloons) in a relatively short period of time. This time period ranges from a few months to several years.

- **Loan-to-value ratio.** You probably want to receive a large cash down payment so that the loan is more secure, while the buyer wants to make a small down payment to retain as much cash as possible. A minimum of 10 percent down is frequently agreed upon.

- **Loan prepayment**. The buyer wants a prepayment privilege, the right to prepay the loan without penalty when new financing can be arranged. You may want this also, to get the money sooner, but unless you have a better use for the money you might prefer that the loan not be paid off early unless there is a prepayment penalty.
- **Interest rate**. This is a good bargaining point. If the rate is below the rate on available loans, expect to get a good price for the property.
- **Right to assign**. With this right, if the initial borrower sells the property during the term of the loan, the new buyer may assume the existing note without the lender's consent. Avoid giving this right unless you are anxious or desperate to sell.
- **Tax considerations**. Periodic payments would result in interest deductions for the borrower each year but taxable income for the note holder.
- **Exculpation**. Is the property the sole collateral for the loan, or is the buyer personally liable to repay the loan? Avoid exculpation. Make the buyer personally liable for the debt.
- **Additional security**. Take whatever additional security is available. If the buyer hasn't sold a former residence, perhaps you can get a second mortgage on that, also.

Seller financing can be fraught with hazards, especially in states that make foreclosure difficult or lengthy for lenders. Offer seller financing only to people you trust and with sound legal documentation.

42

PROCEEDS OF SALE

Your proceeds from the sale of your house is generally the check you receive when you leave the closing. However, you may have to pay income taxes on the gain if you don't meet the reinvestment requirements or the over-age-55 exemption, which are discussed in the next key.

It is important to estimate the proceeds from sale in order to evaluate offers on your property. The highest offer will not bring you the most money when it obligates you to pay many fees and charges. Estimating the proceeds is also important after you have agreed to sell. By carefully estimating what you should receive, you'll be able to notice the possibility of an error on the closing statement and get it fixed before closing. If you wait until closing, under the stress of the moment, you may not be able to detect errors on the closing statement.

To estimate the amount of proceeds, start with the selling price. Subtract the mortgage(s) and other liens on the property. Subtract expenses of sale, including brokerage commissions, legal and title costs, discount points you agreed to pay on the buyer's loan, and so on. A detailed list is on the next page.

SELLER'S ESTIMATED RECEIPTS

ALL FIGURES ARE APPROXIMATE   Date _____

PROPERTY DESCRIPTION	SELLER'S NAME	

		Seller Receives	
SELLING PRICE		$	
OUTSTANDING MORTAGAGES			
1st Mortgage	$		
2nd Mortgage			
Other Encumbrances			
Subtract Total Mortgages .... →		$	
Gross Equity .... →		$	

LESS SELLER'S ESTIMATED EXPENSES	Seller Pays		
Title Insurance Policy	$		
Attorneys Fees			
Release of Lien			
Survey of Property			
Escrow Fees			
Termite Inspection			
Recording Fees			
Brokers Professional Service Fee			
Prepayment Penalty On Loan			
Photographs			
Loan Discount Fee			
Home Warranty			
....			
....			
....			
....			
Total Estimated Expenses .... →		$	
ESTIMATED RECEIPTS .... →		$	

Note:
1. These figures are only estimated and are subject to verification by the Seller.
2. Prorations of taxes, Interest and Insurance are not included on this statement.
3. Our Insurance estimates are based on minimum coverate since types and amounts of coverage varies so much from individual to individual.

Notes: _____

_____

_____

_____

43

INCOME TAX ON SALE OR REINVESTMENT

Form 2119 and Schedule D are used for reporting to the Internal Revenue Service. Instructions to help complete the form are available from the IRS. Most people will find the instructions easy to follow, provided they have kept complete and up-to-date records on the homes they have owned.

Generally, if you paid more for a new principal residence than your old one sold for, the tax on the gain from the sale of the old one is postponed. The relevant figures relate to prices, not equity. For example, suppose your previous house, which was your first house, cost $75,000 two years ago, and you just sold it for $100,000. You paid a $5000 commission and $2000 additional expenses of sale, which are subtracted from the selling price to give a $93,000 amount realized. This is the adjusted sales price. From that, subtract your $75,000 adjusted tax basis (this is a tax term for cost plus capital improvements, less untaxed gains from previous homes) to give an $18,000 gain. This gain will not be taxed provided a new home is purchased for at least $93,000 within two years. See Key 27 on recordkeeping for details of what is included in basis.

If you had paid for fixing-up expenses, you could reduce the cost of the new home by that amount. Fixing-up expenses are narrowly defined. They reduce the needed purchase price of a new home but do not change the amount of gain. *New* is used here to mean new to you, though it could be a very old house that you just bought.

Buying a new house for less than $93,000 will cause some or all of the gain to be taxable. Up to $18,000 will be taxable, depending on the cost of the new home. If the new home cost is $75,000 or less, the entire gain is taxable. If the new home cost is $90,000, then $3000 is taxable and $15,000 deferred.

Whatever the amount of deferred gain, it is not forgiven unless you're over 55 and meet other requirements as described below. The deferred gain carries over to the next house in the form of a carry-over tax basis. The adjusted tax basis of the new home is calculated by subtracting the deferred gain from the previous house(s). For example, suppose your new house costs $120,000. Its adjusted tax basis will be reduced by the $18,000 gain postponed, so it will be $102,000, rather than the $120,000 you paid. If you sold the new one immediately after you bought it, for the same price you paid, you'll have an $18,000 gain, the untaxed amount from the previous house. This illustrates how the untaxed gain from the sale of a house gets built into the new house.

Several items are noteworthy. Since prices are controlling, a taxpayer can leave a transaction with cash. Suppose the old home was owned free and clear so that you get lots of cash from the sale. Then you buy the new one with a small down payment. All of the cash can be kept tax free.

The two-year purchase requirement falls on both sides of the sale. If you sell your old home first, you have two years to buy or build another. If you buy a new home first, you have two years to sell the old one. The time limit is strictly enforced, with military duty as an exception. You are allowed only one transaction every two years, except if the sale was caused by a geographical change in employment (you move at least 35 miles closer to work) for at least 39 weeks.

If you've sold and must file a tax return before you've bought, you need not pay a tax on the gain at that point. When the tax event has occurred, that is, you do buy another or the two-year limit expires, file an amended return for the year of sale.

These provisions apply only to your *principal* residence. They are mandatory—if you buy another principal residence that qualifies for tax deferment, you can't pay a tax on the gain. However, if you buy another residence that is not your principal residence, it does not qualify. A well known government leader missed that point. He sold his home in State X, moved to Washington, D.C., as an elected government official, where he rented. He then bought a home in State Z. He insisted he was still a resident of State X; therefore, the IRS claimed the home in Z could not be a *principal* residence, and he had to pay a tax.

A taxpayer who is over age 55 and has lived in a home for three of the last five years can sell and not pay a tax on all of the built-up gains from the sale of previous residences. This exemption is available only once in a lifetime and must be elected. Further, the election is binding on one's present and future spouse.

44

TAX DEDUCTION
FOR MOVING
EXPENSES

Most of the expenses incurred in home sales and purchases are deductible from gross income as *indirect* moving expenses when the move is related to employment and when distance and employment length requirements are met.

To meet the *distance* test the new principal job must be at least 35 miles farther from the former residence than the old principal job was from the former residence. For example, if the former home was five miles from work, the new job must be at least 40 miles from the former home. In the case of someone returning to full-time work or taking a first job, the principal job location must be at least 35 miles from the former residence.

For an employee to meet the *time* test, he or she must work at least 39 weeks during the 12 months that follows the move. The work can involve more than one employer. A self-employed individual must work at least 39 weeks for the first 12 months and 78 weeks for the two-year period following the move.

Military personnel are exempt from both time and distance requirements when they move because of a permanent change of station. The time test is waived for any employee who:

- Moves to the U.S. because of retirement
- Becomes disabled or dies
- Is transferred for the employer's benefit
- Is laid off, but not for willful misconduct

Moving expenses are deductible even though the tax return is due before the time requirement is met. If the time test is not met, the taxpayer must amend the tax return for the year claimed, or declare the moving expense deducted in one year as other income in the year when the time test was not met. Note that some of the expenses may then be used to increase the tax basis of the home purchased, or to lower the gain on the sale of the previous home.

Deductible moving expenses on the *sale* of a home may include:

- Advertising expenses
- Appraisal fees
- Escrow fees
- Legal expenses (attorney, title, deed preparation)
- Real estate sales commissions
- State fees and other transfer expenses

Expenses related to the sale can be used to reduce the gain instead of being deducted as moving expenses. Since a taxpayer cannot claim both, the deduction as moving expenses is generally preferred because it provides an immediate tax deduction.

Many expenses in connection with the acquisition of a new residence are deductible as moving expenses, provided that the time, distance, and employment tests are met, as described above. These are:

- Appraisal fees
- Escrow fees

- Legal fees
- Points or loan origination charges that are not interest or prepaid interest

These expenses can be added to the adjusted tax basis of the new home, which will reduce the gain upon its resale. As in a sale, a double benefit is not allowed, and most taxpayers prefer to claim a deduction in the current year rather than later.

Indirect moving expenses are limited to certain dollar amounts. There is a $3000 combined total ($6000 for a foreign move) for buying and selling expenses, pre-move house-hunting trips, and temporary living expenses in the new area. All are deductible in full to the limit, except meals, for which the allowance is 80 percent. Of the $3000 limit, a maximum of $1500 ($4500 for foreign) may be deducted for house-hunting and temporary living expenses. Any sale-related expenses that are disallowed because of exceeding the limit may reduce the gain. Similarly, any purchase costs that exceed the limit can increase the basis on the new home.

Direct moving expenses are deductible without limit except for meals which are allowed at 80 percent. Direct expenses include reasonable travel to the new residence and reasonable costs of packing and moving household goods. Storage and insurance for 30 days is allowed. Car travel is allowed at actual costs, or nine cents per mile. Parking fees and tolls are included for either method. The most direct method of travel is required.

Nondeductible items include a loss on the sale of your home, drapery and carpet refitting, club membership fees, or household servant expenses.

Form 3903 is used to report moving expenses, 3903F for foreign moves. Both are available from the Internal Revenue Service.

QUESTIONS AND ANSWERS

Should I buy or rent?

This depends on your individual situation. Are you a permanent resident of an area, or do you expect to move around? Can you afford the down payment and monthly payments involved in buying a house? Is housing affordable in your area? How do rental rates compare to ownership costs? Do you need the tax deductions for interest and real estate taxes? Do you need a hedge against inflation? Are you willing to do home maintenance chores, or to find and direct workers who will do the jobs for you?

If I decide to buy or at least look, should I get a broker to help?

A broker will probably expedite your search not only by showing you many houses in a short time period, but also by providing important information about a community, by preparing contracts, and by arranging financing. Most often, the broker is paid by the seller. However, many individuals prefer to shop by themselves and feel they can strike a better bargain without outside assistance.

What should I look for in a house?

Important considerations are detailed in the keys and checklists offered in this book. Factors include location, interior and exterior suitability, age, and general condition. Affordability and proper financing are essential. You want a house that pleases you and other family members, so it is best to talk it over at length with all concerned.

If I've found a suitable house, how do I proceed?

The next step is to offer a contract. A contract is an enforceable agreement that fixes the rights of the parties involved. Verbal contracts in real estate are not enforceable, so you need something in writing.

Ask your lawyer or broker for advice in preparing a contract. A lawyer will be more expensive but will be working in your best interest, whereas a broker is typically employed and paid by the seller. Using a printed form found in an office supply store is dangerous because few laymen can understand every word of it.

If you want something in the contract—whether it be physical, financial or legal—tell the preparer exactly what it is. Otherwise you and the seller may sign the contract without your important matter being considered.

What are contingencies?

A good contract for the buyer will specify that certain requirements must be met or the deal is canceled. In such cases, the buyer should get a full refund of any earnest money, also called good faith deposit money.

Common contingencies include title, financing, and condition. If the seller can't provide good title, you don't have to buy. And if you can't get the financing specified in the contract, you don't have to buy. If the house is found to be structurally defective or if repair costs exceed a certain dollar amount that the seller won't pay, you can get out of the contract. Other contingencies include making the purchase subject to the sale of your old house, or to the approval of other family members, such as parents, spouse, or even children. You can even put in a clause that if the sun doesn't shine on the day set for closing, you can back out. But those are real weasel words—not to be used by a sincere buyer and not to be accepted by a sensible seller.

What happens after we submit that contract?

The owners can sign and return it, in which case you have a deal, or the owners can return it unsigned. Most commonly, the owners will counteroffer. That is, they will change certain items on the contract you submitted, making it more to their liking, and then initial those changes and return the contract to you. If you initial the changes and return a copy to the owner, the contract is binding. Counteroffers generally bring the contract closer to agreement, but legally they are a rejection of the contract submitted and substitution of another one.

After the contract has been signed, what is the next step?

Clearing contingencies. Typically the buyer arranges physical inspections of the property for termite infestation, mechanical, electrical and plumbing repairs needed, and structural condition. The buyer applies for financing. Behind the scenes the lender checks ownership, appraises the property, and assesses the creditworthiness of the buyer/borrower. This process generally takes from two to 12 weeks, depending on how busy everyone is.

What is a closing?

Also called *settlement* in some places, it is when money and property change hands. Buyer and seller meet across a table, often with their lawyers and a representative from the lending institution and perhaps the title company. The buyer pays the down payment and receives the deed from the seller. The seller leaves with a check. In most situations the deed is left to a lawyer or title company for recordation. The mortgage will also be recorded.

What is recordation?

The courthouse in each county serves as an official place for documents. The clerk of the court, for a small fee, accepts legal documents and places them in official books. This gives 'notice to the world' that certain ownership or certain liens exist.

What if I change my mind about buying?

You can rescind the contract before both parties have signed. If both have signed, read the contract carefully to determine what you're legally liable for. Discuss your intentions with your lawyer. In many cases you'll lose your deposit, but you could lose more or less, depending on what the contract says and the reaction of the seller and broker(s).

How do I sell a house?

You can try yourself, or enlist a broker to help. Selling is a more difficult process than buying, and can be especially trying in a soft market. Often, a reduced price helps effect a quick sale, so you might price it according to your needs for a fast sale.

GLOSSARY

Many of the following terms were adapted from the *Real Estate Handbook* or the *Dictionary of Real Estate Terms*, published by Barron's Educational Series, New York.

Acceptance   agreeing to take an offer; the acceptance of an offer constitutes a contract.

Acre   measure of land containing 43,560 square feet.

Ad valorem tax   tax based on the value of the property.

Adjustable-rate mortgage (ARM)   loan where the interest rate fluctuates according to another rate, as when the mortgage rate is adjusted annually based on the one-year Treasury bill rate, plus a 2 percent margin.

Agency   legal relationship between a principal and agent arising from a contract in which the principal engages the agent to perform certain acts on the principal's behalf.

Agent   one who undertakes to transact some business or to manage some affair for another, with the authority of the latter.

Agreement of sale   written agreement between buyer and seller to transfer real estate at a future date. Includes all the conditions required for a sale.

Amortization   gradual process of reducing a debt in a systematic manner.

Appraisal   an expert's opinion of the value of property arrived at with careful consideration of all available and relevant data.

Appreciation   increase in the value of property.

As is   present condition of property. The "as is" clause is likely to warn of a defect.

Assessed value   value against which a property tax is imposed. The assessed value is often lower than the market value due to state law, conservative tax district appraisals, and infrequent appraisals.

Assignment method by which a right or contract is transferred from one person to another.

Assumable mortgage loan that can be transferred to another party. The transferee assumes the debt, but the original borrower is not released from the debt without a novation.

Balloon mortgage loan having a large final payment.

Balloon payment final payment on a debt.

Bill of sale document used to transfer personal property. Often used in conjunction with a real estate transaction where appliances or furniture are sold also.

Binder brief agreement, accompanied by a deposit, showing intent to follow with a formal contract.

Bridge loan mortgage financing between the termination of one loan and the beginning of another.

Broker one who is licensed by a state to act for property owners in real estate transactions, within the scope of state law.

Brokerage the business of being a broker

Building codes regulations established by local governments describing the minimum structural requirements for buildings; includes foundation, roofing, plumbing, electrical, and other specifications for safety and sanitation.

Cap maximum rate of change of the interest rate on an adjustable-rate mortgage. The mortgage may have an annual or lifetime ceiling.

Capital gain gain on the sale of a capital asset. If long-term (generally over six months), capital gains are sometimes favorably taxed. A personal residence is a capital asset.

Caveat emptor "Let the buyer beware." An expression once used in real estate to put the burden of an undisclosed defect on the buyer. This concept has been eroded in most states.

Chattels   personal property.

Closing   date when buyer and seller exchange money for property.

Closing costs   various fees and expenses payable by the seller and buyer at the time of a real estate closing (also termed *Transaction costs*). Included are brokerage commissions, discount points, title insurance and examination, deed recording fees, and appraisal fees.

Closing statement   accounting of funds from a real estate sale, made to both the seller and the buyer separately. Most states require the broker to furnish accurate closing statements to all parties to the transaction.

Cloud on title   outstanding claim or encumbrance that, if valid, would affect or impair the owner's title.

Commission   1. amount earned by a real estate broker for his services. 2. official state agency that enforces real estate licensing laws.

Commitment letter   written pledge or promise; a firm agreement, often used to describe the terms of a mortgage loan that is being offered.

Common elements   in a condominium, those portions of the property not owned individually by unit owners but in which an indivisible interest is held by all unit owners. Generally includes the grounds, parking areas, maintenance areas, recreational facilities, and external structure of the building.

Community property   property accumulated through joint efforts of husband and wife and owned by them in equal shares. This doctrine of ownership now exists in Arizona, California, Idaho, Louisiana, Nevada, New Mexico, Texas, and Washington State.

Comparables   properties that are similar to the one being sold or appraised. Used in the market approach to appraisal.

Competitive market analysis   an estimate of what a property might bring based on the sale or offering of similar properties, usually by a real estate salesperson. Contrast *Appraisal*.

Conditional offer one that requires certain condition(s) to be fulfilled, such as rezoning of the property or the buyer's need to sell another property, before the contract is binding.

Conditional sales contract written agreement for the sale of property stating that the seller retains title until the conditions of the contract have been fulfilled. See *Contract for deed*.

Condominium system of ownership of individual units in a multiunit structure, combined with joint ownership of commonly used property (sidewalks, hallways, stairs, etc.). See *Common elements*.

Consideration anything of value given to induce entering into a contract; it may be money, personal services, or love and affection.

Contingency condition that must be satisfied before the party to a contract must purchase or sell.

Contract agreement between competent parties to do or not to do certain things for a consideration. Common real estate contracts are contract of sale, contract for deed, mortgage, lease, listing, deed.

Contract for deed real estate installment sales arrangement whereby the buyer may use, occupy, and enjoy land, but no deed is given by the seller (so no title passes) until all or a specified part of the sale price has been paid. Same as *Land contract, Installment land contract, Conditional sales contract*.

Contract of sale same as *Agreement of sale*.

Conventional loan, mortgage 1. mortgage loan other than one guaranteed by the Veterans Administration or insured by the Federal Housing Administration. See *VA loan, FHA loan*. 2. fixed-rate, fixed-term mortgage loan.

Cooperative type of corporate ownership of real property whereby stockholders of the corporation are entitled to use a certain dwelling unit or other units of space. Special income tax laws allow the tenant stock-holders to deduct interest and property taxes paid by the corporation.

Curtesy right of a husband to all or part of his deceased wife's realty regardless of the provisions of her will. Exists in only a few states.

Deed written document, properly signed and delivered, that conveys title to real property. See *General warranty deed, Quitclaim deed, Special warranty deed.*

Deed of trust instrument used in many states in lieu of a mortgage. Legal title to the property is vested in one or more trustees to secure the repayment of the loan.

Deed restriction clause in a deed that limits the use of land.

Default failure to fulfill an obligation or promise, or to perform specified acts.

Deficiency judgment court order stating that the borrower still owes money when the security for a loan does not entirely satisfy a defaulted debt.

Department of Housing and Urban Development (HUD) U.S. government agency established to implement certain federal housing and community development programs.

Depreciation 1. in accounting, allocating the cost of an asset over its estimated useful life. 2. in appraisal, a charge against the reproduction cost (new) of an asset for the estimated wear and obsolescence. Depreciation may be physical, functional, or economic.

Discount points amounts paid to the lender (often by the seller) at the time of origination of a loan, to account for the difference between the market interest rate and the lower face rate of the note.

Dower under common law, the legal right of a wife or child to part of a deceased husband or father's property. Compare *Curtesy.*

Down payment amount one pays for property in addition to the debt incurred.

Due-on-sale clause provision in a mortgage that states that the loan is due upon the sale of the property.

Earnest money deposit made before closing by a purchaser of real estate to evidence good faith.

Easement right, privilege, or interest that one party has in the land of another. The most common easements are for utility lines.

Encroachment building, a part of a building, or an obstruction that physically intrudes upon, overlaps, or trespasses upon the property of another.

Encumbrance any right to or interest in land that affects its value. Includes outstanding mortgage loans, unpaid taxes, easements, and deed restrictions.

Equity interest or value that the owner has in real estate over and above the liens against it.

Equity loan usually a second mortgage whereby the property owner borrows against the house, based on the value of equity built up by appreciation.

Escrow agreement between two or more parties providing that certain instruments or property be placed with a third party for safekeeping, pending the fulfillment or performance of some act or condition.

Et ux. abbreviation of the Latin *et uxor*, which means "and wife."

Exclusive agency listing employment contract giving only one broker, for a specified time, the right to sell the property and also allowing the owner alone to sell the property without paying a commission.

Exclusive right to sell listing employment contract giving the broker the right to collect a commission if the property is sold by anyone, including the owner, during the term of the agreement. See also *Multiple listing service*.

Execute to sign a contract; sometimes, to perform a contract fully.

Fair market value a term generally used in property tax and condemnation legislation, meaning the market value of a property.

Federal Fair Housing Law federal law that forbids discrimination on the basis of race, color, sex, religion, national origin, handicap, or familial status in the selling or renting of homes and apartments.

Federal Housing Administration (FHA) agency within the U.S. Department of Housing and Urban Development that administers many loan programs, loan guarantee programs, and loan insurance programs designed to make more housing available.

Federal National Mortgage Association (FNMA) corporation that specializes in buying mortgage loans, mostly from mortgage bankers. It adds liquidity to the mortgage market. Nicknamed Fannie Mae, FNMA is owned by its stockholders, who elect 10 of its board of directors. The U.S. president appoints the other five directors.

Fee simple or Fee absolute absolute ownership of real property; the owner is entitled to the entire property with unconditional power of disposition during his life, and it descends to his heirs and legal representatives upon his death.

FHA loan mortgage loan insured by the FHA.

First mortgage mortgage that has priority as a lien over all other mortgages. In cases of foreclosure, the first mortgage will be satisfied before other mortgages.

Fixed-rate mortgage loan on which the interest rate does not change over the entire term of the loan.

Fixtures personal property attached to the land or improvements so as to become part of the real estate.

Foreclosure termination of all rights of a mortgagor or the grantee in the property covered by the mortgage.

General warranty deed deed in which the grantor agrees to protect the grantee against any other claim to title to the property and provides other promises.

Graduated-payment mortgage (GPM) loan requiring lower payments in early years than in later years.

Payments increase in steps each year until the installments are sufficient to amortize the loan.

Grantee   party to whom the title to real property is conveyed; the buyer.

Grantor   anyone who gives a deed.

Gross rent multiplier (GRM)   sales price divided by the contract rental rate.

Growing equity mortgage (GEM)   mortgage loan in which the payment is increased by a specific amount each year, with the additional payment amount applied to principal retirement. As a result of the added principal retirement, the maturity of the loan is significantly shorter than a comparable level-payment mortgage.

Hazard insurance   a form of insurance that protects against certain risks, such as fires and storms.

Homeowners' association   organization of the homeowners in a particular subdivision, planned unit development, or condominium; generally for the purpose of enforcing deed restrictions or managing the common elements of the development.

Homeowner's policy   insurance policy designed especially for homeowners. Usually protects the owner from losses caused by most common disasters, theft, and liability. Coverage and costs vary widely.

Inside lot   in a subdivision, a lot surrounded on each side by other lots, as opposed to a corner lot, which has road frontage on at least two sides.

Joint tenancy   ownership of real estate by two or more persons, each of whom has an undivided interest with the right of survivorship.

Junior mortgage   loan whose claim against the property will be satisfied only after prior mortgages have been repaid. See *First mortgage, Second mortgage.*

Land contract   same as *Contract for deed*

Lien   charge against property making it security for the payment of a debt, judgment, mortgage, or taxes; it is a type of encumbrance. A specific lien is against certain property only. A general lien is against all the property owned by the debtor.

List to give or obtain a listing.

Listing 1. written engagement contract between a principal and an agent, authorizing the agent to perform services for the principal involving the latter's property. 2. record of property for sale by a broker who has been authorized by the owner to sell. 3. property so listed.

Listing agreement, Listing contract same as *Listing* (1).

Loan-to-value ratio (LTV) amount borrowed as a percentage of the cost or value of the property purchased.

Lot and block number method of locating a parcel of land. The description refers to a map of a subdivision that numbers each lot and block.

Market value theoretical highest price a buyer, willing but not compelled to buy, would pay, and the lowest price a seller, willing but not compelled to sell, would accept.

Mechanic's lien lien given by law upon a building or other improvement upon land, and upon the land itself, as security for the payment for labor done and materials furnished for improvement.

Mortgage written instrument that creates a lien upon real estate as security for the payment of a specified debt.

Mortgagee one who holds a lien on property or title to property, as security for a debt; the lender.

Mortgagor one who pledges property as security for a loan; the borrower.

Mortgage banker one who originates, sells, and services mortgage loans. Most loans are insured or guaranteed by a government agency or private mortgage insurer.

Mortgage insurance protection for the lender in the event of default, usually covering 10 to 20 percent of the amount borrowed.

Multiple listing service (MLS) association of real estate brokers that agrees to share listings with one another. The listing broker and the selling broker share the commission. The MLS usually distributes a book with all listings to its members, updating the book frequently. Prospective buyers benefit from the ability to select from among many homes listed by any member broker.

National Association of Real Estate Brokers (NAREB) organization of minority real estate salespersons and brokers who are called *REALTISTS*®.

National Association of *REALTORS*® (NAR) organization of *REALTORS*®, devoted to encouraging professionalism in real estate activities. There are over 600,000 members of NAR, 50 state associations, and several affiliates.

Negative amortization increase in the outstanding balance of a loan resulting from the failure of periodic debt service payments to cover required interest charged on the loan.

Net listing listing in which the broker's commission is the excess of the sales price over an agreed-upon (net) price to the seller; illegal in some states.

Notary public officer who is authorized to take acknowledgments to certain types of documents, such as deeds, contracts, and mortgages, and before whom affidavits may be sworn.

Novation agreement whereby a lender substitutes one party to a contract for another, releasing the original party from any obligation.

Offer expression of willingness to purchase a property at a specified price.

Open house method of showing a home for sale whereby the home is open for inspection on an advertised date.

Open housing condition under which housing units may be purchased or leased without regard for racial, ethnic, color, or religious characteristics of the buyer or tenants.

Open listing listing given to any number of brokers without liability to compensate any except the one who first secures a buyer who is ready, willing and able to meet the terms of the listing or secures the seller's acceptance of another offer. The sale of the property automatically terminates all open listings.

Oral contract unwritten agreement. With few exceptions, oral agreements for the sale or use of real estate are unenforceable. In most states, contracts for the sale or rental of real estate, unless they are in writing are unenforceable under the Statute of Frauds. Oral leases for a year or less are often acceptable.

Performance bond assures that a contractor will perform in accordance with the contract and protects against a breach of contract.

Permanent mortgage mortgage for a long period of time (over 10 years).

Plat plan or map of a specific land area.

Points see *Discount points.*

Prepayment penalty penalty imposed on a borrower when a loan is retired before maturity.

Prepayment privilege right of a borrower to retire a loan before maturity.

Principal 1. one who owns or will use property. 2. one who contracts for the services of an agent or broker; the broker's or agent's client. 3. the amount of money raised by a mortgage or other loan, as distinct from the interest paid on it.

Principal and interest payment (P&I) periodic payment, usually made monthly, that includes the interest charges for the period plus an amount applied to amortization of the principal balance. Commonly used with self-amortizing loans.

Principal, interest, taxes, and insurance (PITI) monthly mortgage payment (P&I), with the addition of an amount deposited in escrow for future payment of taxes and insurance.

Private mortgage insurance (PMI) see *Mortgage insurance.*

Prorate to allocate between seller and buyer their proportionate shares of an obligation paid or due; for example, to prorate real estate taxes.

Purchase-money mortgage mortgage given by a grantee (buyer) to a grantor (seller) in part payment of the purchase price of real estate.

Quitclaim deed deed that conveys only the grantor's rights or interest in real estate, without stating the nature of the rights and with no warranties of ownership. Often used to remove a possible cloud on the title. Contrast with *General warranty deed.*

Real estate 1. in law, land and everything more or less attached to it. Ownership below to the center of the earth and above to the heavens. Distinguished from *personal property.* Same as *realty.* 2. in business, the activities concerned with ownership and use transfers of the physical property.

Real Estate Settlement Procedures Act (RESPA) law that states how mortgage lenders must treat those who apply for federally related real estate loans on property with one to four dwelling units. Intended to provide borrowers with more knowledge when they comparison shop for mortgage money.

REALTIST® member of the National Association of Real Estate Brokers, a group composed primarily of minority brokers.

REALTOR® a professional in real estate who subscribes to a strict Code of Ethics as a member of the local and state boards and of the National Association of REALTORS®.

Redlining illegal practice of refusing to originate mortgage loans in certain neighborhoods on the basis of race or ethnic composition.

Refinance to substitute a new loan for an old one often in order to borrow more or to reduce the interest rate.

Sales contract same as *Contract of sale.*

Second mortgage a subordinated lien on a property created by a mortgage loan over the amount of a *first mortgage.*

Self-amortizing mortgage loan that will retire itself through regular principal and interest payments. Contrast with *Balloon mortgage.*

Seller's market economic conditions that favor sellers, reflecting rising prices and market activity.

Settlement same as *Closing.*

Special assessment assessment made against a property to pay for a public improvement by which the assessed property is supposed to be especially benefited.

Special warranty deed deed in which the grantor limits the title warranty given to the grantee to anyone claiming by, from, through, or under him, the grantor. The grantor does not warrant against title defects arising from conditions that existed before he owned the property.

Specific performance legal action in which the court requires a party to a contract to perform the terms of the contract when he has refused to fulfill his obligations. Used in real estate, since each parcel of land is unique.

Subcontractor one who performs services under contract to a general contractor.

Subdivision tract of land divided into lots or plots suitable for home-building purposes. Some states and localities require that a subdivision plat be recorded.

Subject to mortgage arrangement whereby a buyer takes title to mortgaged real property but is not personally responsible for the payment of any portion of the amount due. The buyer must make payments in order to keep the property; however, if he fails to do so, only his equity in that property is lost.

Survey   process by which a parcel of land is measured and its area ascertained; also, the blueprint showing the measurements, boundaries, and area.

Sweat equity   value added to a property due to improvements as a result of work performed personally by the owner.

Term, amortization   for a loan, the period of time during which principal and interest payments must be made; generally, the time needed to amortize the loan fully.

Title   evidence that the owner of land is in lawful possession thereof; evidence of ownership.

Title insurance   insurance policy that protects the holder from loss sustained by defects in the title.

Title search   examination of the public records to determine the ownership and encumbrances affecting real property.

Veterans Administration (VA)   government agency that provides certain services to discharged servicemen.

VA loan (mortgage)   loan that is guaranteed by the United States Veterans Administration. Discharged servicemen with more than 120 days of active duty are generally eligible for a VA loan, which typically does not require a down payment.

Vendee   buyer.

Vendor   seller.

Warranty deed   title to real estate in which the grantor guarantees title. Usually protects against other claimants, liens, or encumbrances and offers good title.

Zoning ordinance   act of city, county, or other authorities specifying the type of use to which property may be put in specific areas. Examples: residential, commercial, industrial.

CHECKLISTS AND TABLES

A good checklist is a useful device to try to ensure that nothing has been overlooked. Although a perfect home has yet to be built, a checklist may help determine whether a house has so many negatives that it is unsuitable for you, or if it has a 'fatal flaw'—something you wouldn't want to own at any price. Use the list to help jog your memory about each feature.

Using the payment tables, you will be able to determine the amount that will be payable monthly on your mortgage.

General Checklist

Address _____

Date(s) shown _____

Shown by _____

Owner's name _____

Phone numbers _____

Reason for selling _____

Availability
 or
Urgency of sale _____

Age _____ Asking price _____

Special financing
or other terms _____

Taxes and fees_____

Heating/cooling costs _____

Builder _____ Stories or levels _____

Style & special features _____

Construction quality Interior: _____

 Exterior: _____

Comments

Location Characteristics

	Superior	Average	Inferior
School district			
Elementary			
Junior high			
High			
Parochial			
Fire and police protection			
Transportation			
Medical facilities			
Shopping			
Recreational facilities			
Religious			
Neighborhood			
Subdivision			
Homeowners' ass'n			
View			

Other

Interior Arrangements

	Superior	Average	Inferior
Number of bedrooms Closet(s) size, shelving			
Number of bathrooms Size, fixtures, floor			
Kitchen size & layout			
Kitchen equipment			
Living room			
Family room			
Laundry/utility room			
Floor plan			
Floor coverings			
Window treatments			
Built-in cabinets			
Paint			
Wallpaper			
Fireplace			
Basement			
Heating/cooling plant			

Additional Comments

House Exterior Checklist

	Superior	Average	Inferior
Roof			
Facade			
Windows			
Doors			
Drainage			
Paint			
Garage (size, attached)			
Attic			
Storage			

Additional Comments

Lot Checklist

	Superior	Average	Inferior
Size			
Fence			
Shrubbery			
Trees			
Lawn			
Sprinklers			
Swimming pool			
Hot Tub			
Patio			
Driveway			
Traffic			
View			
Zoning			
Flood plain			
Environmental hazards			

Additional comments

Servicing Checklist

	Superior	Average	Inferior
Waste (Sewer, septic)			
Heating			
Air conditioning			
Insulation			
Ceiling			
Walls			
Weather-stripping			
Storm windows, doors			
Wiring			
Plumbing			
Appliances			

Additional Comments

Negotiating Checklist

Asking price _____

Probable price _____

Financing _____

Points _____

Closing costs:

  Legal _____

  Recording _____

  Appraisal _____

Inspections:

  Inside _____

  Outside _____

  Pests _____

Contingencies:

  Sale of old house _____

  Mortgage approval _____

  Mortgage terms _____

Additional Comments

Financing Checklist

Existing financing

Assumability _____

Lender(s) _____

Unpaid balance(s) _____ Remaining term _____

Interest rate _____ Balloon or other payments due _____

Transfer fees _____

Prepayment penalty _____

New financing

Lender name and phone	Type	Rate	L-T-V Term	Points	Fees	Lock-in

Monthly Principal and Interest Payments
per $1,000 of Principal

Term (Years)	Contract Interest Rate (%)			
	7.00	7.25	7.50	7.75
1	86.53	86.64	86.76	86.87
2	44.77	44.89	45.00	45.11
3	30.88	30.99	31.11	31.22
4	23.95	24.06	24.18	24.30
5	19.80	19.92	20.04	20.16
6	17.05	17.17	17.29	17.41
7	15.09	15.22	15.34	15.46
8	13.63	13.76	13.88	14.01
9	12.51	12.63	12.76	12.89
10	11.61	11.74	11.87	12.00
11	10.88	11.02	11.15	11.28
12	10.28	10.42	10.55	10.69
13	9.78	9.92	10.05	10.19
14	9.35	9.49	9.63	9.77
15	8.99	9.13	9.27	9.41
16	8.67	8.81	8.96	9.10
17	8.40	8.54	8.69	8.83
18	8.16	8.30	8.45	8.60
19	7.94	8.09	8.24	8.39
20	7.75	7.90	8.06	8.21
21	7.58	7.74	7.89	8.05
22	7.43	7.59	7.75	7.90
23	7.30	7.46	7.61	7.77
24	7.18	7.34	7.50	7.66
25	7.07	7.23	7.39	7.55
26	6.97	7.13	7.29	7.46
27	6.88	7.04	7.21	7.37
28	6.80	6.96	7.13	7.30
29	6.72	6.89	7.06	7.23
30	6.65	6.82	6.99	7.16

Monthly Principal and Interest Payments
per $1,000 of Principal

Term	Contract Interest Rate (%)			
(Years)	8.00	8.25	8.50	8.75
1	86.99	87.10	87.22	87.34
2	45.23	45.34	45.46	45.57
3	31.34	31.45	31.57	31.68
4	24.41	24.53	24.65	24.77
5	20.28	20.40	20.52	20.64
6	17.53	17.66	17.78	17.90
7	15.59	15.71	15.84	15.96
8	14.14	14.26	14.39	14.52
9	13.02	13.15	13.28	13.41
10	12.13	12.27	12.40	12.53
11	11.42	11.55	11.69	11.82
12	10.82	10.96	11.10	11.24
13	10.33	10.47	10.61	10.75
14	9.91	10.06	10.20	10.34
15	9.56	9.70	9.85	9.99
16	9.25	9.40	9.54	9.69
17	8.98	9.13	9.28	9.43
18	8.75	8.90	9.05	9.21
19	8.55	8.70	8.85	9.01
20	8.36	8.52	8.68	8.84
21	8.20	8.36	8.52	8.68
22	8.06	8.22	8.38	8.55
23	7.93	8.10	8.26	8.43
24	7.82	7.98	8.15	8.32
25	7.72	7.88	8.05	8.22
26	7.63	7.79	7.96	8.13
27	7.54	7.71	7.88	8.06
28	7.47	7.64	7.81	7.99
29	7.40	7.57	7.75	7.92
30	7.34	7.51	7.69	7.87

Monthly Principal and Interest Payments per $1,000 of Principal

Term (Years)	Contract Interest Rate (%)			
	9.00	9.25	9.50	9.75
1	87.45	87.57	87.68	87.80
2	45.68	45.80	45.91	46.03
3	31.80	31.92	32.03	32.15
4	24.88	25.00	25.12	25.24
5	20.76	20.88	21.00	21.12
6	18.03	18.15	18.27	18.40
7	16.09	16.22	16.34	16.47
8	14.65	14.78	14.91	15.04
9	13.54	13.68	13.81	13.94
10	12.67	12.80	12.94	13.08
11	11.96	12.10	12.24	12.38
12	11.38	11.52	11.66	11.81
13	10.90	11.04	11.19	11.33
14	10.49	10.64	10.78	10.93
15	10.14	10.29	10.44	10.59
16	9.85	10.00	10.15	10.30
17	9.59	9.74	9.90	10.05
18	9.36	9.52	9.68	9.84
19	9.17	9.33	9.49	9.65
20	9.00	9.16	9.32	9.49
21	8.85	9.01	9.17	9.34
22	8.71	8.88	9.04	9.21
23	8.59	8.76	8.93	9.10
24	8.49	8.66	8.83	9.00
25	8.39	8.56	8.74	8.91
26	8.31	8.48	8.66	8.83
27	8.23	8.41	8.58	8.76
28	8.16	8.34	8.52	8.70
29	8.10	8.28	8.46	8.64
30	8.05	8.23	8.41	8.59

Monthly Principal and Interest Payments
per $1,000 of Principal

Term	Contract Interest Rate (%)			
(Years)	10.00	10.25	10.50	10.75
1	87.92	88.03	88.15	88.27
2	46.15	46.26	46.38	46.49
3	32.27	32.38	32.50	32.62
4	25.36	25.48	25.60	25.72
5	21.25	21.37	21.49	21.62
6	18.53	18.65	18.78	18.91
7	16.60	16.73	16.86	16.99
8	15.17	15.31	15.44	15.57
9	14.08	14.21	14.35	14.49
10	13.22	13.35	13.49	13.63
11	12.52	12.66	12.80	12.95
12	11.95	12.10	12.24	12.39
13	11.48	11.63	11.78	11.92
14	11.08	11.23	11.38	11.54
15	10.75	10.90	11.05	11.21
16	10.46	10.62	10.77	10.93
17	10.21	10.37	10.53	10.69
18	10.00	10.16	10.32	10.49
19	9.81	9.98	10.14	10.31
20	9.65	9.82	9.98	10.15
21	9.51	9.68	9.85	10.02
22	9.38	9.55	9.73	9.90
23	9.27	9.44	9.62	9.79
24	9.17	9.35	9.52	9.70
25	9.09	9.26	9.44	9.62
26	9.01	9.19	9.37	9.55
27	8.94	9.12	9.30	9.49
28	8.88	9.06	9.25	9.43
29	8.82	9.01	9.19	9.38
30	8.78	8.96	9.15	9.33

Monthly Principal and Interest Payments
per $1,000 of Principal

Term (Years)	Contract Interest Rate (%)			
	11.00	11.25	11.50	11.75
1	88.38	88.50	88.62	88.73
2	46.61	46.72	46.84	46.96
3	32.74	32.86	32.98	33.10
4	25.85	25.97	26.09	26.21
5	21.74	21.87	21.99	22.12
6	19.03	19.16	19.29	19.42
7	17.12	17.25	17.39	17.52
8	15.71	15.84	15.98	16.12
9	14.63	14.76	14.90	15.04
10	13.77	13.92	14.06	14.20
11	13.09	13.24	13.38	13.53
12	12.54	12.68	12.83	12.98
13	12.08	12.23	12.38	12.53
14	11.69	11.85	12.00	12.16
15	11.37	11.52	11.68	11.84
16	11.09	11.25	11.41	11.57
17	10.85	11.02	11.18	11.35
18	10.65	10.82	10.98	11.15
19	10.47	10.64	10.81	10.98
20	10.32	10.49	10.66	10.84
21	10.19	10.36	10.54	10.71
22	10.07	10.25	10.42	10.60
23	9.97	10.15	10.33	10.51
24	9.88	10.06	10.24	10.42
25	9.80	9.98	10.16	10.35
26	9.73	9.91	10.10	10.28
27	9.67	9.85	10.04	10.23
28	9.61	9.80	9.99	10.18
29	9.57	9.75	9.94	10.13
30	9.52	9.71	9.90	10.09

Monthly Principal and Interest Payments per $1,000 of Principal

Term (Years)	Contract Interest Rate (%)			
	12.00	12.25	12.50	12.75
1	88.85	88.97	89.08	89.20
2	47.07	47.19	47.31	47.42
3	33.21	33.33	33.45	33.57
4	26.33	26.46	26.58	26.70
5	22.24	22.37	22.50	22.63
6	19.55	19.68	19.81	19.94
7	17.65	17.79	17.92	18.06
8	16.25	16.39	16.53	16.67
9	15.18	15.33	15.47	15.61
10	14.35	14.49	14.64	14.78
11	13.68	13.83	13.98	14.13
12	13.13	13.29	13.44	13.59
13	12.69	12.84	13.00	13.15
14	12.31	12.47	12.63	12.79
15	12.00	12.16	12.33	12.49
16	11.74	11.90	12.07	12.23
17	11.51	11.68	11.85	12.02
18	11.32	11.49	11.66	11.83
19	11.15	11.33	11.50	11.67
20	11.01	11.19	11.36	11.54
21	10.89	11.06	11.24	11.42
22	10.78	10.96	11.14	11.32
23	10.69	10.87	11.05	11.23
24	10.60	10.79	10.97	11.16
25	10.53	10.72	10.90	11.09
26	10.47	10.66	10.84	11.03
27	10.41	10.60	10.79	10.98
28	10.37	10.56	10.75	10.94
29	10.32	10.52	10.71	10.90
30	10.29	10.48	10.67	10.87

Monthly Principal and Interest Payments
per $1,000 of Principal

Term (Years)	Contract Interest Rate (%)			
	13.00	13.25	13.50	13.75
1	89.32	89.43	89.55	89.67
2	47.54	47.66	47.78	47.90
3	33.69	33.81	33.94	34.06
4	26.83	26.95	27.08	27.20
5	22.75	22.88	23.01	23.14
6	20.07	20.21	20.34	20.47
7	18.19	18.33	18.46	18.60
8	16.81	16.95	17.09	17.23
9	15.75	15.90	16.04	16.19
10	14.93	15.08	15.23	15.38
11	14.28	14.43	14.58	14.73
12	13.75	13.90	14.06	14.21
13	13.31	13.47	13.63	13.79
14	12.95	13.11	13.28	13.44
15	12.65	12.82	12.98	13.15
16	12.40	12.57	12.74	12.91
17	12.19	12.36	12.53	12.70
18	12.00	12.18	12.35	12.53
19	11.85	12.03	12.20	12.38
20	11.72	11.89	12.07	12.25
21	11.60	11.78	11.96	12.15
22	11.50	11.69	11.87	12.05
23	11.42	11.60	11.79	11.97
24	11.34	11.53	11.72	11.91
25	11.28	11.47	11.66	11.85
26	11.22	11.41	11.60	11.80
27	11.17	11.37	11.56	11.75
28	11.13	11.32	11.52	11.71
29	11.09	11.29	11.48	11.68
30	11.06	11.26	11.45	11.65

Monthly Principal and Interest Payments per $1,000 of Principal

Term (Years)	Contract Interest Rate (%)			
	14.00	14.25	14.50	14.75
1	89.79	89.90	90.02	90.14
2	48.01	48.13	48.25	48.37
3	34.18	34.30	34.42	34.54
4	27.33	27.45	27.58	27.70
5	23.27	23.40	23.53	23.66
6	20.61	20.74	20.87	21.01
7	18.74	18.88	19.02	19.16
8	17.37	17.51	17.66	17.80
9	16.33	16.48	16.63	16.78
10	15.53	15.68	15.83	15.98
11	14.89	15.04	15.20	15.35
12	14.37	14.53	14.69	14.85
13	13.95	14.11	14.28	14.44
14	13.60	13.77	13.94	14.10
15	13.32	13.49	13.66	13.83
16	13.08	13.25	13.42	13.59
17	12.87	13.05	13.22	13.40
18	12.70	12.88	13.06	13.24
19	12.56	12.74	12.92	13.10
20	12.44	12.62	12.80	12.98
21	12.33	12.51	12.70	12.88
22	12.24	12.43	12.61	12.80
23	12.16	12.35	12.54	12.73
24	12.10	12.29	12.48	12.67
25	12.04	12.23	12.42	12.61
26	11.99	12.18	12.38	12.57
27	11.95	12.14	12.34	12.53
28	11.91	12.10	12.30	12.50
29	11.88	12.07	12.27	12.47
30	11.85	12.05	12.25	12.44

Monthly Principal and Interest Payments
per $1,000 of Principal

Term	Contract Interest Rate (%)			
(Years)	15.00	15.25	15.50	15.75
1	90.26	90.38	90.49	90.61
2	48.49	48.61	48.72	48.84
3	34.67	34.79	34.91	35.03
4	27.83	27.96	28.08	28.21
5	23.79	23.92	24.05	24.19
6	21.14	21.28	21.42	21.55
7	19.30	19.44	19.58	19.72
8	17.95	18.09	18.24	18.38
9	16.92	17.07	17.22	17.37
10	16.13	16.29	16.44	16.60
11	15.51	15.67	15.82	15.98
12	15.01	15.17	15.33	15.49
13	14.60	14.77	14.93	15.10
14	14.27	14.44	14.61	14.78
15	14.00	14.17	14.34	14.51
16	13.77	13.94	14.12	14.29
17	13.58	13.75	13.93	14.11
18	13.42	13.60	13.78	13.96
19	13.28	13.46	13.65	13.83
20	13.17	13.35	13.54	13.73
21	13.07	13.26	13.45	13.64
22	12.99	13.18	13.37	13.56
23	12.92	13.11	13.30	13.49
24	12.86	13.05	13.25	13.44
25	12.81	13.00	13.20	13.39
26	12.76	12.96	13.16	13.35
27	12.73	12.92	13.12	13.32
28	12.70	12.89	13.09	13.29
29	12.67	12.87	13.07	13.27
30	12.64	12.84	13.05	13.25

Monthly Principal and Interest Payments
per $1,000 of Principal

Term	Contract Interest Rate (%)			
(Years)	16.00	16.25	16.50	16.75
1	90.73	90.85	90.97	91.09
2	48.96	49.08	49.20	49.32
3	35.16	35.28	35.40	35.53
4	28.34	28.47	28.60	28.73
5	24.32	24.45	24.58	24.72
6	21.69	21.83	21.97	22.11
7	19.86	20.00	20.15	20.29
8	18.53	18.68	18.82	18.97
9	17.53	17.68	17.83	17.98
10	16.75	16.91	17.06	17.22
11	16.14	16.30	16.46	16.63
12	15.66	15.82	15.99	16.15
13	15.27	15.43	15.60	15.77
14	14.95	15.12	15.29	15.46
15	14.69	14.86	15.04	15.21
16	14.47	14.65	14.83	15.01
17	14.29	14.47	14.65	14.84
18	14.14	14.33	14.51	14.69
19	14.02	14.20	14.39	14.58
20	13.91	14.10	14.29	14.48
21	13.82	14.01	14.20	14.40
22	13.75	13.94	14.13	14.33
23	13.69	13.88	14.07	14.27
24	13.63	13.83	14.02	14.22
25	13.59	13.79	13.98	14.18
26	13.55	13.75	13.95	14.15
27	13.52	13.72	13.92	14.12
28	13.49	13.69	13.89	14.09
29	13.47	13.67	13.87	14.07
30	13.45	13.65	13.85	14.05

INDEX